AESTHETIC LEGACIES

In the series

THE ARTS AND THEIR PHILOSOPHIES

edited by Joseph Margolis

Aesthetic Legacies

LUCIAN
KRUKOWSKI

Temple University Press
Philadelphia

Temple University Press, Philadelphia 19122

Published 1992
Printed in the United States of America

∞ The paper used in this publication meets the minimum requirements of American National Standard for Information Sciences—Permanence of Paper for Printed Library Materials, ANSI Z39.48–1984

Library of Congress Cataloging-in-Publication Data
Krukowski, Lucian, 1929–
Aesthetic legacies / Lucian Krukowski.
p. cm. — (Arts and their philosophies)
Includes bibliographical references and index.
ISBN 0-87722-972-4 (hard)
1. Kant, Immanuel, 1724–1801—Aesthetics. 2. Shopenhauer, Arthur, 1788–1860—Aesthetics. 3. Hegel, Georg Wilhelm Friedrich, 1770–1831—Aesthetics. 4. Aesthetics, Modern—19th century. 5. Aesthetics, Modern—20th century. 6. Modernism (Aesthetics) 7. Postmodernism.
I. Title. II. Series.
BH191.K78 1992
111'.85'09034—dc20 92-19307

To my parents

Contents

Preface ix
Introduction 1

I. The Aesthetic Systems

CHAPTER ONE. Kant 19
CHAPTER TWO. Schopenhauer 41
CHAPTER THREE. Hegel 65

II. Themes and Transformations

CHAPTER FOUR. Kant and Taste 89
CHAPTER FIVE. Schopenhauer and Expression 104
CHAPTER SIX. Hegel and Progress 118

III. Modernism and Postmodernism

CHAPTER SEVEN. Form, Intention, Criticism 135
CHAPTER EIGHT. Three Dogmas of Modernism 172
CHAPTER NINE. The Postmodern Legacy 189

Notes 225
Index 241

Preface

THE NOTION of "legacy" is, in the main, a comforting one. It gives a sense of continuity, a connectedness between past, present, and a manageable future that makes its actual receipt a welcome prospect. Taken this way, a legacy is a gift that is also deserved, and it carries only the condition that one use it well, and pass it on to others who are rather more than less like oneself—for this is the agreement that purports to civilize historical process. Accepting a legacy supposes that one can use what one gets, and it also supposes that the givers, back down the line, will not be used badly—oh, recast and rearranged perhaps, but still recognized for their efforts and the virtues they pass one.

But comfort and continuity are not the sole determinants of the world, and so, legacies are not always welcome. For at certain times the obligations they insist on outweigh the benefits they contain. Continuity is not a virtue at those times when one is ashamed of one's parents and angry at one's sibs. The reasons, whether such history is familial or universal, are usually about the failures of the past—the failure to see what has become evident and to act on the evidenced needs. But it is also evident that every present needs some past or other. So when antagonism to a given legacy is substantial, then that past need not be entirely rejected; rather, it can be inverted, its values becoming the vices one then strives against. In this way, the present is spared the task of constructing itself from scratch.

The legacies we construe as our past emerge from a field that, from any present vantage, looks clear and ordered in some parts and indistinct or unsubstantial in others. By and large, the ordered parts are the ones to which we attach the causal claims for how we are. But this also says that "how we are" determines the past we order—or take as ordered. Of course, the past is not just what we make (of) it; it is stubbornly there in the guise of its accounts and artifacts. But just as stubbornly, we sort through these to find ones that support the values upon which we, as we say, have built the present. Fortunately, however persuasive our present appears (and however clear its past), we are never sure but that some shadow in the historical field hides a richer or truer legacy, or some veniality in the one we have. The need to search these out moves us on again; it is what constitutes our future.

The tension between these senses of "legacy"—accepting and rejecting, finding and ordering—is the general theme of this book. I approach my primary concerns—the aesthetics of modernism and postmodernism—through certain theoretical legacies I trace to origins in the philosophies of Kant, Schopenhauer, and Hegel. To trace a legacy is to identify certain themes that document the changing values between successive periods. Such themes exemplify, through changes in their own designation, the sequence of descriptive and normative accounts that identifies a legacy's historical journey. So, for example, one of the themes I trace originates in the Kantian aesthetic of "beauty" and shows its historical development in the guise of "taste" and, then, "form." Another theme has its source in Schopenhauer's concept of "will," and continues as "expression" and "intention." My third theme, fittingly, originates in the Hegelian context of "spirit," and follows this through "progress" into "criticism." Each of these names identifies a value that characterizes the aesthetic at a particular time, yet the order of succession shows the changes in value that link times with each other. How these linkages are understood, the mix of acceptance and rejection—supplementation or inversion—that marks their successive stages, is a central part of my subject.

Through the themes I thus select and trace, I develop a certain narrative of the interaction between art and ideology from the mid-eighteenth century through the moment of this writing. I say "certain" here because evidently there are other themes and narratives of transformation. I do not offer mine as "comprehensive"—for I do not agree with the politics of that notion—but I do believe my narrative to be evocative, which assessment, in turn, comes not from any achievement of a "dispassionate gaze" but from what, after a considerable time, has become the clearest location of my own history.

I reached my first maturity in the second part of modernism, and have since been living through its as yet unfinished transition into postmodernism. What first attracted me to this way of life were the values in which the art was then centered, values that, so it seemed, could equally be applied to the world's recalcitrance and my own timidities. This was a legacy from the first part of modernism. It proposed that without question art is important, and that such importance is not—should, could not be—confined to art's own provenance. This normative generosity, which here I take to be both a defining and limiting characteristic of modernism, eventually waned as praxis, and my interest turned to the question of its theoretical origins.

Each of the legacies I have chosen originates as an aspect of a comprehensive philosophical system. The "importance" I speak of is not to be found in the specifically aesthetic formulation but in the work it does in the overall philosophical argument—the place, if you will, assigned the aesthetic in the formulation of reality. Of course, this last notion now seems overblown, but in the historical period here at issue, the extravagance shows itself in philosophy's incorporation of art as both subject and mechanism, an incorporation that underlies such more recent claims as that art "reveals," "expresses," "anticipates," "admonishes," its own time. Some of my friends now say that it (art) never was such; others say it is no longer. But however this may be (and it, too, is a matter of legacy), the negation of this claim of art's importance is itself important, for it continues the tracing of my chosen themes through—and past—modernism, and into the present.

I have been asked why, methodologically, I did not first identify the themes I take to characterize postmodernism and then trace them back through recursive historical stages to whatever point I establish as their origins. But the present has too much information; the "blooming and buzzing" of its incessant presentations makes it all too easy to manifest that irritating symptom of postmodernism—the confusion of immediacy with clarity. This is a symptom that, now in retrospect, is more like a "feature," and more illuminating than irritating—but it was not so beforehand. So, in this writing, I rejected the hermeneutic strategy for a different approach. At the outset, it seemed to me that our difficulties with the roles given the aesthetic in the philosophies of Kant, Schopenhauer, and Hegel are of a kind with difficulties we were having with the ideologies of modern art. I thought to test this by assuming each philosophy as a point of origin and then seeing—as the saying goes—how one might get from there to here. Specifically, I wanted to see if an analysis of how the aesthetic functions in each philosophy could be moved out of its systematic origins and construed as an ideological legacy extending into modernism. I also wanted to see whether, in the course of tracing this evolution, the similarities and differences among these aesthetics could be projected onto similarities and differences in artistic style. Characterizing these intersections—among styles, and between style and theory—would then constitute an interpretation of modernism.

In the early stages of this writing, I was not sure how far beyond modernism I wanted to extend this tracing. At a certain point, however, it seemed to me that postmodernism, whatever else it might be, was as strong a repudiation of modernist values as was the modernist affirmation of the legacies through which it rejected the alternative academic values of its own past. Given this, the evident next step was to formulate the affirmative values in postmodernism. So I continued my tracing, this time from the late, "dogmatic" phase of modernism, as far as I could reach into the present. This second tracing proceeds through experiences of a more recent past: the geographical dissemination of art-culture, the challenges to received modernist ideologies and institutions, and the first scattered formulations of alternatives in both practice and theory. These are experiences that I bring together into an interpretation of postmodernism—one that, given its vantage in the present of this period, will no doubt change between the writing and printing of this book.

My debts are the same now as in past writings: family, friends, colleagues, and memories of these; I acknowledge them all. I do wish to give special thanks to Joseph Margolis who, early on, identified my effort as one of "accretion" and gently urged me to rewrite and expand earlier drafts.

A paper in which I formulated some central issues in this book appeared in *VIA* 10 (1990), under the title "Art and Ethics in Kant, Hegel, and Schopenhauer." Portions of the discussion on Tolstoi and Barthes in Chapter Seven appeared in the *British Journal of Aesthetics* (Spring

1990), under the title "Artist-Work-Audience: Musings on Barthes and Tolstoi." An early version of Chapter Eight was presented at the International Congress on the Philosophy of Art held in Lahti, Finland, in 1990, and printed in the proceedings of the congress.

AESTHETIC LEGACIES

Introduction

1. ORIGINS

THIS IS a study of aesthetic themes in transformation. I locate these themes in the philosophies of Kant, Schopenhauer, and Hegel and then trace them through their ideological impact on the periods we know as modernism and postmodernism. My choice of both themes and origins is governed by my sense that, together, they encompass the main ambitions of aesthetic theory during that historical span. These ambitions are first tested by the roles assigned to aesthetics in the respective philosophical systems: how, for Kant, the appreciation of beauty seeks to impart a metaphysical "wholeness" to the separate cognitions of nature and morality; how Schopenhauer assigns artistic creativity the task of imaging the noumenal principle of "will"; and how Hegel sees artworks as exemplifications of "progress" in history. The later ambitions—the transformations—of these aesthetic themes move from systematic philosophy into a more direct concern with art, particularly the art of modernism. Here, the task is primarily one of elucidating the various claims of the new art: the claim, for example, that formal excellence is the achievement that best characterizes art, or that expression is both the reason and content of artistic activity, or that art functions as a critical rebuke to the historical malingering of the social order. As my narrative proceeds, the further transformations of these aesthetic themes signal the advent of postmodernism. I identify the impetus for this move as a turn in modernist ideology in which once-radical values are commodified and institutionalized. This is a turn of belief into dogma, and the reaction to it begins with an inversion of modernist values and continues with the first articulations of a distinctly new ideology. This brings us to our present, and I conclude my study with an analysis of what I take to be the emerging characteristics of this time.

2. DEVELOPMENT

For modern readers, the aesthetic theories of the eighteenth and nineteenth centuries often sound grandiose and unsustainable. There are many reasons for this: One is the impact of analytic philosophy with its general rejection of speculative methodology and, particularly, its rejection of metaphorical language in philosophical discourse. Another reason, an extension of the first, is our present unwillingness to assign art the task of fulfilling such encompassing ideals as these earlier philosophies demand—such ideals as "synthesizing" or "penetrating" or "exemplifying" the principle subject of the overall system. Despite such cautions, however, it is also not surprising that the period and theories in question increasingly come to attract our attention. Indeed, one of the inducements they give for our returning to them *is* the centrality there of the role of aesthetics in the general concerns of philosophy.

Our interest in the role aesthetics plays in these earlier philosophical systems can be piqued by contrasting this role with the peripheral one that is generally accorded aesthetics today—particularly in those studies where the task is to show how symbols veridically represent the world. Art is not usually counted among veridical symbols these days, and this shift in attitude is dramatized when we notice that it begins at the historical point where art generally loses its instrumentality in philosophical system making. This shift coincides with another one—equally important to my thesis—when art gains its independence from those cultural services and obligations that, previously, had identified it as a "profession." Both these shifts introduce the period we know as modernism.

Despite the new problematics of art's social role, and despite its diminished stature as a subject of philosophical concern, art did not suffer an ideological neglect in this transition; to the contrary, its interpretations, explanations, narratives, reconstructions, deconstructions, have increased exponentially since the turn of the century. But this new theorizing was directed at an art that presented itself as free of external obligations, an art that is autonomous and unified—a "modern" art. In the modernist context, interpretations of art have largely paralleled art's claim to self-sufficiency by avoiding reference to philosophical theories about how the world is and how we know it to be. When art's practical need for autonomy came to demand that its semantics be directed at worlds of its own making, its theories followed suit. This corollary between theory and practice needs a first emphasis here: The theoretical counterpart of art's new social autonomy is the rejection in aesthetic theory of the extravagances of Romanticism and idealism—of such notions, for example, as that the world expressed by art is "better" than the actual one, or that the world of artistic representations is the world as it "really" is. Perhaps, also, this posture of autonomy had become strategically useful: Rather than fight on the old worn terrain of idealism, or the new hostile terrain of positivism, modernist aesthetic theory disavowed art's instrumentality for epistemic or ontological issues—except as these concern art's self-cognition. This disavowal actually became a strategy of consolidation: The range of aesthetic concerns moves away from nature and comes to coincide with the realm of art—thus giving aesthetics the insular safety of its own subject.

This consolidation, this carving out of a common domain for both theory and subject was not, however, without its dangers. The doctrinal stability of aesthetics, in its new role as apologist for the historical development of its subject, became vulnerable to the vicissitudes and eccentricities of artworks—especially to such works as threaten the needed distinctness of the realm of art. And artworks, in turn, became vulnerable to the inconsistencies between their descriptions and their practices—to the growing irrelevance of the self-definition to which they continued to formally respond. These vulnerabilities, as my narrative shows, presage the decline of modernism.

The early twentieth-century estrangement of aesthetics from philosophy was not, in fact, particularly debilitating to either side. For aesthetic theory, the new subject—modern art—demanded increasing attention to that art's ideological needs and cultural battles. The pattern that developed here for both art and its theory was holistic and extravagant, and it stood in strong contrast to the logical, compartmentalizing rigor that characterized analytic philosophy. But one should note that earlier philosophy—as exemplified by the protagonists of this study, Kant, Schopenhauer, and Hegel—can also be seen as extravagant and holistic. Indeed, it can be argued that the systematic ambitions of nineteenth-century philosophy require a variety of extravagant theses: the assumption, as in Kant, of a priori forms of cognition that "underlie" but do not depend on empirical knowledge; Schopenhauer's presentation of his metaphysical system through the irreconcilable accounts of will and representation; Hegel's assurance that all matters of fact can be accounted for through teleological explanation. In my discussion, I suggest that these philosophical extravagances are taken over by twentieth-century art—appropriated as a rightful inheritance—through a transformation of certain ideas, or "themes," that move out of their philosophical origins into the aesthetic ideologies of modernism. One theme is found in the claim that art is formally autonomous and yet effective as an instrument of social change; another follows the sources of artistic creativity into regions of primal process and irrationality; yet another is found in the aesthetic holism implied by the thesis "unity of the arts." I develop these themes, their extensions, and their disavowals in the course of this study.

3. ISSUES

My recursion to nineteenth-century origins, at first glance, may seem a nostalgic approach to aesthetic theory. But nostalgia is neither my taste nor my aim here, for I believe that uncovering certain linkages between then and now can clarify our present difficulties in theorizing about art. Some of these difficulties come out of having assigned our immediate past—modernism—to a historical past, a period we no longer consider ourselves part of. Where we are now is often called postmodernism, and this dependent term does point to our uncertainties about where it is we are. I do not have an alternative term to propose here; indeed, given the popularity of this usage, another term may not be needed. But I do have something to say about the theoretical uncertainties. One of my aims in tracing present aesthetic beliefs back to their nineteenth-century origins is to show that certain implications of their early role in systematic philosophy did not survive the journey through modernism.

I describe the transition from modernism to postmodernism as a turn from belief to dogma. It is a transition marked by the domestication of extravagance—by a manipulation of popular ideas and images that, a few decades earlier, was barely thinkable for art. This transition also contains currents of disbelief—in the received narratives and values of art history, and in the aesthetic self-sufficiency of the arts. One consequence of all this is that art is created in ways that are so stylistically expedient as to make inconsistency a virtue. Aesthetic theory has lagged behind practice in accounting for this and too often comforts itself with the supposition that our time of transition is also an interim period between high styles. I argue against this and present a more consequential view of postmodernism.

My study begins with a commentary on the aesthetic theories of Kant, Schopenhauer, and Hegel. One reason for this choice of protagonists is that, in their very different ways, they saw the comprehensive realm of the aesthetic as having great philosophical importance. Understanding what these respective "aesthetics" contain, and what they imply, can put our own views in a new light: We might find out what we now no longer believe about art—although we may still think we do—and this in turn could show us how modernism has become historical.

One belief I have in mind is about what art requires us—artists and audience—to be like in order for it, art, to function as we want it to. Another way of putting this is to ask what effects creating and appreciating, properly done, have on those involved and, by extension, on the greater society. My way of showing what "requires" and "properly done" come to is to trace these notions back to the relation between aesthetic theory and the other philosophical doctrines of Kant, Schopenhauer, and Hegel. Through this comparison, I indicate how each philosopher identifies the nature of the aesthetic and assigns it a particular philosophical task. These assignments mirror the specific conciliations between the world and its knowledge in each philosophy that, in turn, lead to each philosopher's conception of the work of art: what he wants such works to be like, what is required for their creation, and what is proper to their appreciation. In this regard, I also ask how the concept of moral agency is related to the aesthetic theory in each case—whether the criteria that determine what it is to be an ethical person have any place in the requirements for the making and appreciating of art as these are personified, respectively, by the artist and the audience.

4. SOURCES

Here, I offer a brief overview of the aesthetic theories of Kant, Schopenhauer, and Hegel. This serves as a guide to the direction my analysis will take in the first three chapters of this study.

The central issue in Kant's aesthetics is appreciation—the exercise of "taste"—for he sees this as providing a link between understanding and reason, between empirical knowlege and moral obligation. The subject of appreciation is beauty, primarily the beauty of nature. By reflecting on its harmonies we find signs that the noumenal world—nature as it is behind its appearances—is a rational one, and this gives us the hope that our moral "ought" is compatible with nature's "is." The beauties of art, in their individual ways, merely confirm and elaborate on this hope. Kant's ideal of appreciation—the person with "good taste"—is a paradigm for his moral individual: Both are able to view the world apart from personal interest, the first in order to see the harmonies in beauty that are ordinarily obscured by considerations of utility, the second in order to separate the imperatives of duty from the motives of prudence or desire.

Knowledge of noumenal reality in Schopenhauer's philosophy does not have the provisional cast of a Kantian reflection; this reality, which he calls the will, can be known directly. But such knowledge, given the irrational nature of the will, merely gives us reason to avoid its impositions—and we do this best through contemplation and withdrawal. Schopenhauer identifies art as the philosophical instrument that penetrates the world's conventional surface to provide knowledge of this reality, and it is the creative act—more so than appreciation—that is central to Schopenhauer's aesthetic. The images of art present the things of the world as they would be if free of the will's ceaseless demands: a world of essences modeled on the Platonic "forms." The artist, however, has the role of both knowing and expressing this world and, therefore, cannot join the philosopher's retreat into the contemplation of its essences. This tension between action and knowledge underlays Schopenhauer's characterization of creative expression: the artist as seer who is, at the same time, psychically oppressed and socially alienated. But this characterization is not entirely negative. The artist's condition is also a condition of philosophical truth.

For Kant, history is a hope; for Schopenhauer it is an illusion; but for Hegel it is the process through which world and thought become adequate to each other. This process is teleological: It progresses toward an end, and this end is a final synthesis of all duality. Hegelian thought is replete with examples of such dualities: God and the world, good and evil, mind and things, individuals and society. History, specifically the history of culture—from its exotic origins in the ancient east to the particular fusion of Christianity and reason in Hegel's own Germany—is the stage upon which these dualities are played out and overcome. The common thread in this overcoming, the central characteristic of Hegel's teleology, is the ascendancy of spirit over matter; and our own representations of reality—art, religion, philosophy—both document and embody this ascendancy.

Kant's aesthetic places primary emphasis on nature, in whose unencumbered beauties he finds the hint of its noumenal rationality. Schopenhauer divides nature between actuality and ideal and gives art the task of finding the latter in the former. Hegel's aesthetic concerns are with art, not nature, for he sees nature as the repository of "inert matter," as an irrational hindrance to the "evolution of spirit." For Hegel, the history of art is a document of the history of culture and shows culture's progress from primitivism to rationality. The images of art show a corresponding evolution from the material dependency of animism, through patterns of illusionistic refinement, to the conceptual freedom of poetic discourse.

5. THEMES AND TRANSFORMATIONS

The function of the aesthetic, however differently construed in each of these theories, remains in the service of the philosophical system. In all three, the aesthetic has an epistemic function: It tells us something philosophically important about the world that we could not obtain in any other way. When these epistemic claims are discarded as, by and large, they have been in modern times, the more purely aesthetic values remain. But because they no longer are measured by their contributions to systematic philosophy, these values become internal to their specific subject—the interpretation of art.

In Part I of my study I show how systematic philosophical concerns determine the ways in which the questions of aesthetics are formulated and, in turn, how answers to these questions contribute to the completeness of each system. In Part II, I isolate and formalize these answers, and thereby separate them from their originary functions.

This separating out of aesthetic theory is in keeping with its changing role in the nineteenth and twentieth centuries where the study of art and beauty becomes a matter for specialists: aestheticians, critics, art historians. The thesis that art uniquely contributes to our knowledge of the world is discounted, and other values supplant epistemic ones as the concerns of aesthetics and art theory.

When inquiry moves from the philosophical function of the aesthetic to the problems of art, certain characteristics emerge in each aesthetic theory that can be considered apart from their origins. This indicates a first separation between aesthetics and the parent system, and the beginning of its role as autonomous theory. I identify these characteristics as specific "themes," which I call "taste," "expression," and "progress," and in Part II, I trace the historical transformation of these themes out of their sources in the aesthetics of Kant, Schopenhauer, and Hegel into a position of doctrinal self-sufficiency. Here, I comment briefly on each.

"Taste" is a matter of response to the aesthetic, and it raises the question of capacity and how it is achieved. Specifically, this is the Kantian question about the practice of appreciation and its relationship to our other—nonaesthetic—capacities, that is, our empirical and moral judgments. While the exercise of taste places certain constraints upon the act of aesthetic perception, upon the judgment that something is beautiful, it also comes to identify certain characteristics of things that are the proper subjects of this perception. While Kant's emphasis is on the perception, this "externalizing" of taste moves the theme into a further transformation where it becomes a demarcator of formal properties central to all artworks. The emphasis on form then becomes a new aesthetic value.

"Expression" is a function of creativity, and it both characterizes and justifies artistic process. When artistic expression exemplifies cosmic process—as Schopenhauer has it—then its value remains epistemic: It tells us something important about the world. When it is viewed as an intensified function of personality, then the expressive result—the artwork—points inward and tells us something about our own selves that we need to know. We are then constrained to go through the artifact to its source in the creative psyche—the intention of the artist—and this effort moves the theme of expression into a further transformation. The creative process then discards its metaphysical task of mirroring the will and takes up the task of self-expression—acquiring along the way the romantic images of alienation. Later, these very images, through a doctrinal rehabilitation of creativity and its sources, become a model for psychic and social well-being.

"Progress," as a teleological concept, imposes inevitability onto change. It also has a normative sense—that the direction of change is for the good. Traditional construals of art resist this second sense, for the value of artistic masterworks needs to be corroborated, not reduced, as they recede into the past. Hegel layers these conflicts in interpretation one upon the other, and the thesis of "progress in art" takes on credibility when it goes beyond its purely aesthetic sense—when artworks are understood not only through their internal, art-historical relationships but as symbols of progress in culture. In this way, the changing images of art take on value as they exemplify the stages of historical progress. At a later point, this thesis of art as cultural exemplification takes an exhortatory turn when art's symbolic capacities are seen to move faster than do the other forms of its culture. The aesthetic theme of "progress" then assumes a critical stance, and this marks its further transformation.

In Chapter Seven, I shift my discussion from the concerns indicated by the terms "taste," "expression," and "progress," and I trace their thematic development into a further stage: aesthetic theory as polemical justification for radical style in art. This, as I argue, marks the shift away from the speculative aesthetics of the nineteenth century into the ideologically centered aesthetics of modernism. To document this shift, a change of signifiers is needed, and I offer a second set of terms that I take to be a conceptual progeny of the first set but that better fits these new—exhortatory and critical—purposes. The terms are: "form," "intention," and "criticism."

The transition from "taste" to "form" identifies what we have come to know as "formalist aesthetics." Here, an artwork's distinctly aesthetic characteristics are located in the interplay of its structural components. As befits the Kantian origins of this theme, other characteristics of artworks—such as mimetic or descriptive power, or utility—are normatively discounted. This presents formalist theory with the dual obligation of showing how one separates out formal characteristics from all others in the appreciation of traditional art, and how one dismisses these others from consideration in the creation of new art. The austerity of the demand this places on both artist and audience is echoed by another demand: that the emphasis on form in aesthetics be recognized as a propaedeutic for social value—the correlation between formal autonomy and social freedom.

The transition from "expression" to "intention" traces the creative process from its origins in Schopenhauer's will, through its location in the workings of artistic genius, into its acceptance as a source of communal well-being. In this transition, the creative act comes to supersede the artwork as locus of aesthetic value, and realization of that value entails a recursion from work to its source in the artist's intention. In this way, the search for aesthetic value in the origins of the expressive impulse redirects appreciation from the work of art to the creative process.

In its historical setting, the conflation of artistic expression with the stigmas of deviance and neurosis has art reveal hidden truths about the irrationalities of nature and the human psyche; and the capacity to reach and configurate such truths is restricted to the singular person of "genius." Under later, more benign interpretations, tapping the sources of expression comes to be seen as propaedeutic to psychological health and the openness of social frameworks. Artworks, here, function as testimonials to this achievement, and "making art" becomes a familiar and accepted social practice.

The transition from "progress" to "criticism" affirms its Hegelian legacy of the telic nature of historical process, but it also points at the growing estrangement of stylistic development in art from the realities of its cultural matrix. When cast as cultural symbols, artworks present the form of telic possibility to society, and discrepancies between symbol and actual achievement give the artwork a critical function. Both formal and expressive characteristics of artworks take on a critical cast when social beliefs become incompatible with the appreciation of new works. Novelty, in a teleological framework, is the aesthetic signal of progress and, thereby, of value; and the failure to appreciate the novel in art portends a social stagnation. The Hegelian task of countering this stagnation becomes the agency of the artistic "avant-garde." In a later turn, art-as-criticism declines as a value when the novelty of artworks no longer underwrites the demand that appreciation examine the premises of its culture.

6. TOWARD THE PRESENT

In the last two chapters of this study, I trace the process of thematic transformation still further—from the early stages of modernism into its decline, and through this into the period we now call postmodernism. My account of modernist ideology attributes its polemical nature to a disjunction between aesthetic ideals and the values of the social order. I characterize the decline of modernism as a rejection of the ideals—the normative implications—of its ideology while at the same time promoting the purely aesthetic appeal of its images. This deletion of ideology from image signals the turn from belief into dogma. It creates a situation in which the polemical basis of modernist theory is rejected through the argument that its goals have been achieved and must now be consolidated. The dogmatic turn in theory is thus justified by appeal to conservation of value. In practice, this often entails the political—in this case, art-political—rejection of extended versions of the very theory to which it, the dogma, nominally subscribes. Dogma, of course, is the antagonist of theory. It rejects the fragility of theory, its susceptibility—indeed, openness—to transformation, even to its own replacement.

I take the fear of theoretical self-replacement to be both symptom and cause of the transition from modernism to postmodernism. It is the fear that theory would unwittingly extend itself to practices that deny it its position as arbiter of practice. This fear is compounded when such practices present themselves as indifferent to the identity given them by theory and to the social position this identity implies. Modernist theory qua dogma fears its extension to artworks, for example, that do not care to be "fine," or that have more urgent agendas than the aesthetic. One way for such theory to protect itself against these fears is by historically encapsulating its subject, and relegating further events to another realm, with which it need not be concerned. This strategy leads to the "end of art," a historical reading of artistic process whose emerging popularity in late modernism signals, in my view, the advent of postmodernism.

The evident fact that art has continued beyond the time of its "end" need not—although it may—denigrate the value of such art, but it does suggest some new readings. The onset of postmodernism is more a reaction against ideology than against imagemaking, and accordingly, this further transformation of aesthetic themes does not so much identify a new style as new ways of theorizing. "Art's end" may be an opportune thesis for devaluating the art of postmodernism, but it can also be used to bring modernist values into question. Of the values I associate with modernism, I take the following to be the most vulnerable: (*a*) the "autonomy" of art—the thesis that art, qua art, has its own ontological and normative history, and that its cogent interpretations are only by reference to this history; and (*b*) the "unity" of art—the thesis that the particular arts share certain characteristics that are constitutive of their status as art and, as such, outweigh all considerations of extra-artistic affinities. The rejection of these modernist theses takes the form of such counterproposals—or "inversions"—as the following: (*c*) Artworks function to represent the interests of the social groups of their origins, and the effectiveness of such representations is undermined by the thesis—and the politics—of "artistic autonomy"; and (*d*) such distinctions as those between "fine" and "popular" art, or between "art" and "nonart," weaken the strategies and denigrate the constituencies of the new art. I take these counterproposals to indicate some of the characteristics and theoretical interests of postmodern art.

The last chapter of this study brings my tracing of aesthetic themes into the present. Because the subject is closest in time, it generates, paradoxically, the most speculative part of my discussion: Here I try to find—but not impose—a form in the bewildering variety of present practices in art. This impress of variety, as I see it, proceeds not only from my lack of historical distance, it points to a genuine decentralization of the arts. The new allegiances I describe are not between individual artworks and a historical concept or paradigm of art. Rather, they are between things, activities, and places, casually or occasionally called art, and the interests, needs, ambitions, and historical wounds of socially diverse groups. Postmodern art is directed at promoting interests, filling and fullfilling needs and ambitions, and supporting strategies to compensate for wounds. None of these functions works the same way in every group, although some do overlap; and the artworks in question do not conform to any orthodoxies of style or method—although there are distinctions that can be made.

In discussing postmodernism, it is easier to show what it is not, through its contrast with modernism, than to identify its own emerging characteristics. As my narrative proceeds, I attempt to do both, however, thus giving my thematic progression a sense, although tentative, of completeness. I do not offer new names for this last transformation of themes—as neither my perceptions of things nor the things themselves seem as yet ready for such commitment. My narrative ends with an account of some recent controversies between the arts and public policy that, as they play out, could set the conditions for new names to emerge.

I
THE AESTHETIC SYSTEMS

ONE

Kant

1. AESTHETIC AND NONAESTHETIC

SOME OF the importance, and difficulty, of Immanuel Kant's aesthetic theory can be understood by placing it in the context of his overall philosophical system. The *Critique of Judgment,*[1] which is the main locus of this theory, has often been characterized as a bridge between the concerns of the *Critique of Pure Reason* and the *Critique of Practical Reason,* between the analysis of how the understanding organizes sense data into contingent empirical judgments,[2] and the argument for the necessary and universal—although nonempirical—nature of moral judgments.[3] It seems clear that Kant's efforts in the third *Critique* to synthesize these concerns, which earlier he had so carefully separated, are due to the realization that an ontology in which fact and value are so sundered is vulnerable to skepticism: On the one hand, we would have a rationally grounded moral code that demands an obedience for which we can find no justification in our perceptions of the world; and on the other hand, our systematizations of nature would provide no guarantees that nature is or will continue to be as our perceptions show it to be. The task Kant reserves for the aesthetic judgment is to provide a sensate basis for rationality and, through this, to save empirical judgments from being reduced to mere instrumentalism, while also protecting moral judgments from the charge of arbitrariness. It is in this sense that one can characterize Kant's third *Critique,* particularly his analyses of beauty and sublimity, as an argument against skepticism—a skepticism as would stem from the theoretical isolation of morality from empirical knowledge. Remarkably, Kant entrusts this crucial argument to the realm of aesthetics, thus giving the study a new prominence in eighteenth-century philosophy as well as setting the stage for the sometimes extravagant claims made for it in the nineteenth century. I will introduce two versions of these later claims in the discussions of Schopenhauer and Hegel in subsequent chapters.

Kant's argument, in summary form, goes as follows: Aesthetic appreciation is revelatory; it provides sensory evidence that the organization of nature is rational in a way analogous to the organization of our rational faculties. This evidence is found either directly in the perception of natural beauty or indirectly through the symbolic representation of nature in art. Importantly, however, what appreciation tells us does not, in the strict sense, constitute knowledge about the world. The aesthetic judgment, unlike empirical and moral judgments, is not based on laws, and, thus, is not determinate. The evidence that beauty provides can only be reflected upon.

In Kant's first *Critique,* events are explained through their determination by natural laws; in the second *Critique,* human actions are regarded as autonomous under the concept of freedom. Kant presents the problem of their interrelationship in this way: "Now even if an immeasurable gulf is fixed between the sensible realm of the concept of nature and the supersensible realm of the concept of freedom . . . just as if they were two different worlds of which the first could have no influence upon the second, yet the second is *meant* to have an influence on the first. The concept of freedom is meant to actualize in the world of sense the purpose proposed by its laws, and consequently nature must be so thought that the conformity to law of its forms at least harmonizes with the possibility of the purposes to be effected in it according to laws of freedom."[4] In the third *Critique,* Kant provides us with reason to believe in the possibility of a harmony between natural laws and the laws of freedom. He does this by dividing the appreciation of beauty into four parts: The evidence of harmony is found in the appearance of purpose in nature, the sense of unity and totality we perceive in the relationship of parts—its *purposiveness.* The perception that provides this evidence is a special (aesthetic) kind marked by its freedom from either empirical or practical concerns with its subject—it is *disinterested.* Our judgment that nature has the appearance of purpose justifies our theoretical need for compatibility between nature and freedom; as this form of judgment ought not to sustain exceptions, we consider it to be *necessary.* Because our motive for this judgment is the desire for theoretical completeness rather than the satisfaction of subjective interest, we consider it as holding without exception for all rational beings and, thus, as *universal.* Kant identifies these four—purposiveness, disinterestedness, necessity, and universality—as the "moments" of aesthetic judgment; they are the conditions that must be satisfied in order for appreciation to be aesthetic, whether it is directed toward nature or art. Kant organizes these moments according to the categorical scheme of the first *Critique:* Purposiveness refers to the formal characteristics identified by the judgment, to their "relationship"; disinterestedness refers to the characteristics of the judgment itself, to their "quality"; necessity refers to the strength of the judgment's claim on our beliefs, to its "modality"; and universality refers to the scope of the judgment, to its "quantity."[5]

One philosophical consequence of our judging that nature appears purposive is the strengthening of our belief that good reasons for right actions *can* be found in appearances: that we—all of us—ought to act morally because such actions are in conformity with the way things are. But Kant hedges this conclusion in an important sense, and his doing so limits the program, and the achievements, of the aesthetic judgment. In the context of the overall critical system, the third *Critique* is not a full partner with the other two because it has an epistemic limitation that the others do not: Aesthetic appreciation does not tell us anything about how the world is, only how we hope it is; and the rules that guide appreciation are only exemplary—they cannot be empirically demonstrated, nor can they rationally demand our agreement. Kant stipulates that the findings of the aesthetic judgment are not assertions; we cannot know them to be true—we can only regard them "as if" they were.[6] In this sense, "purposiveness" is only an image of purpose; "disinterestedness" remains a psychological ideal of perception; and, consequently, the "necessity" and "universality" ascribed to the judgment are only subjective aspirations for completeness and, therefore, not logically binding. This limitation, our inability to assert that nature gives us sensory evidence of the unity and purpose indicative of a rational plan, is the limitation that Kant places on all of philosophy. This limitation is seen in his theory of nature through his denial that we can have noumenal knowlege, knowledge of the world that underlies our perceptions, the world "as it is in itself";[7] and it is also seen in his moral theory where he places explanation of how freedom is possible, the "causality of freedom," beyond the outer limits of metaphysics proper.[8] However, Kant denies aesthetics even the limited epistemic authority he gives to empirical and moral judgments, for these latter do generate laws, and are thus "determinate," while aesthetic judgment remains a rumination on their separate findings and, thus, "reflective."[9] Nevertheless, this greater limitation does not make the aesthetic judgment worthless. Although we cannot know that things are as they appear, certain appearances—the beauties of art and nature—give us reason to hope that nature and our perceptions are in accord. This hope encourages us to believe that our empirical knowledge, partial and contingent as it may be, is progressively accurate in its description of the world's totality; and this belief, in turn, encourages us to hope that there is a correspondence between the moral imperatives that guide our actions and the structure of nature.

2. AESTHETIC FUNCTIONS AND AESTHETIC SUBJECTS

I now turn from this general view to a more specific look at Kant's aesthetics. By examining his treatment of certain concepts that are central to aesthetic theory, I propose to identify the theme—or "legacy"—which in the following parts I trace through later ideologies. The concepts I have in mind can be specified through their division into pairs: The first pair, "appreciation-creativity," identifies aesthetic functions; the second pair, "nature-art," identifies aesthetic subjects. I approach the distinctions in the first pair by showing how Kant describes the actions that typify each component: appreciation by the function of "taste," and creativity by "genius." In considering the second pair, I ask how its subjects, nature and art, manifest the values that Kant specifies for the aesthetic judgment: the values of "beauty" and "sublimity." Kant locates the "judging" of the aesthetic judgment primarily in the appreciation of beauty. He does not actually use the term "appreciation"; instead, he identifies "the faculty of judging of the beautiful" through the exercise of "taste."[10] I discuss some special implications and peculiarities of this term in Chapter Four, but for present purposes I equate taste with appreciation and use this term to contrast the function of creativity. In the "Analytic of the Sublime," Kant identifies creativity, the creation of art, with the person and special capacities of "genius." Here, I extend Kant's thesis and interpret genius as a manifestation of the "natural sublime" occurring through human agency. I justify this interpretation through the account Kant gives of both: the metaphors with which he indicates that creativity has—indeed, requires—the selfsame characteristics of force, boundlessness, freedom, as do nature's more extravagant manifestations. Sublimity and creativity, unlike beauty and appreciation, are primarily evidenced as actions: The storm displaces the still harmonies of lansdcape with its urgencies, and the artist's act overrides the stabilities of taste-governed rules. This reading of the Kantian sublime presumes to extend the influence of his aesthetic theory beyond the formalism with which he is usually associated to theories of creativity and expression.[11]

The tensions that emerge when considering the pairings in the third *Critique*—nature-art, beauty-sublimity, appreciation-creativity—speak to the complexities of Kant's synthesizing effort. Undoubtedly, Kant did not think of these as basic antagonisms but as oppositions that extend and stabilize the architecture of his overall system; this, after all, is the point of the effort. Yet, some of Kant's influence on later aesthetic theory is found in the persistence of these distinctions *as* antagonisms, and it is also found in later ideological demands that choices be made between the components of each pair. Thus, as I show in later chapters, theories emerge that respectively champion taste, or creativity, or the work of art, as the central value for aesthetics.

In order to pursue this general path of inquiry, one first needs to understand how these distinctions work for Kant, to elucidate each, and then follow it to the others. My first question, accordingly, is how Kant applies the aesthetic judgment to nature and art, how one might understand the philosophical role he assigns to the appreciation of beauty in each, and the role he assigns to the creation of art. I want to determine whether there is a difference in the philosophical value of these appreciations—whether, for Kant's theoretical purposes, nature or art is the more fitting subject, and how appreciating and creating each contribute to these purposes.

In the *Critique of Judgment,* Kant devotes the entire first section, the "Analytic of the Beautiful," to the nature of aesthetic appreciation, yet he relegates the nature of artistic creativity to one part of the smaller second section on the "Analytic of the Sublime." These alliances—between appreciation and beauty, and creation and sublimity—are suggestive, and worth pursuing. I propose here that Kant locates philosophical value primarily in the *appreciation* of beauty, not in its making. This proposal gives the following thrust to Kant's theory: (*a*) Done properly, appreciation provides us with the capacity to affirm the continuity between contingent empirical knowledge and the necessity of moral law; creativity, as it relies on an innate disposition or "talent," merely produces the images of such continuity. (*b*) Appreciation is a capacity that can be learned and developed and, in this respect, it is like the capacity for moral action; creativity, as it is innate, is not subject to the correctives of volition. The first point refers to the mediating role that appreciation plays in empirical and moral cognitions, but it leaves open the question whether any such role is played by the creation of art. The second point refers to the compatibility that appreciation has with philosophical analysis, and thus to the possibility that we can *all* learn how to appreciate beauty. The capacity to make art, on the other hand, seems relegated to a few extraordinary individuals.

These considerations show that the aesthetic judgment has not only theoretical but practical value. Practically, the appreciation of beauty takes on the universality Kant requires of moral imperatives by evoking the possibility of a universal agreement on matters of taste: Individuals who claim unity through agreement on the moral law can recognize this unity through a shared sensibility. With this evocation of a sensory-rational continuum, the appreciation of beauty provides morality with the hope that it (too) will eventually be successful in acquiring the free assent of *all* individuals to its laws—the eventual fusion of "ought" and "is." This reveals one of the theoretical purposes of Kant's third *Critique:* to provide a way of justifying the rational demands of moral imperatives through sensory agreement on taste. In this way, the aesthetic judgment diminishes morality's need to find its reasons in a transcendent, legislating deity.[12]

Although Kant emphasizes the philosophical importance of appreciation, he makes a distinction between the subjects that are most properly called beautiful and others to which the term either applies with reservations or not at all. It is revealing that one of Kant's favored exemplars of natural beauty is landscape, and it is worth noting why this is so.[13] The landscape of Kant's choice is one that is neither contrived nor unruly: neither the one that has been clipped and pruned into artifactual submission nor the one in which parts and whole are indiscriminately and unendingly entangled. Such a balanced landscape is particularly suited to aesthetic appreciation because its qualities do not resist transformation into the cognitive symbols, ordinarily in opposition, of design and freedom. Kant identifies and delimits these wanted qualities of landscape through a measure much like the classical Greek "avoidance of excess." Beautiful nature, from Kant's historical perspective, is the Greek ideal become Enlightenment landscape. Design and freedom are harmonized through temperance, and thus, the classical notion of "beauty" as the image of the "good" is moved, by Kant, to a decidedly nonclassical locus: the image of a "natural ordering" provided by landscape.[14]

Now, these characteristics of Kant's ideal landscape can be seen as directly analagous to those that identify both the practice and subject of appreciation. Proper appreciation requires a soul that maintains its harmony when free of prudential interests, and its proper subject maintains its formal integrity in the absence of any signs of its utility. The intersection of these values makes the ideal of beauty actual.

3. CLASSIFICATION OF THE ARTS

This alliance between natural beauty and appreciation does not go so far as to exclude art from Kant's aesthetic. For him, art is a kind of travelogue within the realm of nature that provides access to the varieties of beauty beyond the range of direct individual experience. Although the images of art and nature both provide us with semblances of rationality, and thus reinforce the authenticity of our moral experience, they do so in different ways. Beautiful nature is consequent upon proper appreciation; the beauties in art depend on creative work. But this is not the kind of work that is associated with the production of utilitarian objects. Kant describes art as "production through freedom, i.e., through a will that places reason at the basis of its actions."[15] While the whole of nature can be referred, in a speculative sense, to the workings of a (divine) will, we otherwise understand natural processes as mechanical or instinctual, and the beauty that we find in their effects is given its holistic form by our mediated perception—the requirements of aesthetic judgment. Works of art, on the other hand, are mediated—given holistic form—through the volitions required for the creative act—the workings of genius. Aesthetic appreciation, when it encompasses both nature and art, has a double task: to find a symbol for the harmonies of nature in the made unity of the artwork and then to return to nature and find in it the expanded analogue of artistic beauty.

Kant places a limiting set of conditions on the characteristics of artworks that are similar to those he places on aesthetic appreciation. In both contexts, the aim is to safeguard freedom, or "autonomy." The central value of the artwork is in its form—that characteristic internal relation of parts through which unity is projected. The peripheral values include both practicalities and pleasures—the uses to which works are put and the sensory gratifications they provide us. Created form is central to art in the same sense that formal purposiveness is central to beauty in nature. Appreciation of the former extends the scope of appreciation in the latter, and the wanted analogy between them depends on the same absence of constraints in each domain. Such constraints, as found in utility and possession, are present in artifacture to an inevitably greater degree than in nature. For art to overcome its artifactual limitations and maintain its value as "fine," that is, "free" art, these constraints must be minimized: Utility undermines purposiveness, and possession compromises disinterestedness, and both inhibit the "free play of the imagination"—which, after all, gives aesthetic form its proper subject.

Kant presents us with a categorical schema—a "division"—of the arts that, as I will show, is somewhat rudimentary when compared with Schopenhauer and Hegel. Nevertheless, Kant does present certain formal grounds for differentiating between the arts, and he also grades them according to their capacities and limitations for his philosophical purposes. Kant's basic division is between the *arts of speech*, the *formative arts*, and the arts of the *play of sensations*. Each of these is then further subdivided.[16] The first division, speech, encompasses the arts of "poetry" and of "rhetoric." This does not actually constitute a pairing, however, for Kant echos Plato's attack on the Sophists by accusing rhetoric of deceptively promising knowledge and providing only entertainment. However, Kant does not follow Plato in extending this accusation to poetry, for he accords poetry the capacity of providing "food" and, thereby, "life" to conceptual understanding. Although both poetry and rhetoric deal with the stuff of the imagination, the aesthetically fatal dishonesty of the latter's intentions serves to expel it from the category of fine arts within which, for systematic reasons as it seems, it was first included. Poetry, because of its "innocence," escapes condemnation; and because it bypasses the senses and appeals directly to the imagination, Kant ranks it highest of all the arts.[17]

The second division, the formative arts, further divides into the arts of "sensible truth" and "sensible illusion," the former comprising architecture and sculpture, and the latter painting and landscape gardening. The term "truth" here is somewhat misleading, for Kant uses it only to distinguish visual images that also include tactility from those that do not—the familiar distinction between two-dimensional and three-dimensional artforms. However, Kant considers three-dimensionality, although more "true" because physically concrete, to place a limit on imaginative freedom, and thus, he ranks painting highest in this division. In his assessment of architecture he identifies a more serious limitation: The utilitarian aspect of architecture, that aspect which it shares with the category of "craft," compromises its full status as a fine art. Here, the "art-craft" distinction, so central to later idealist aesthetics, is given an important early formulation. Curiously, Kant's judgment that architectural forms that admit to utilitarian criteria cannot be entirely free is not applied to the art of landscaping, which, although three-dimensional and often utilitarian, he considers of a piece with the illusionistic form of painting. In this regard, Kant finds the persuasiveness of illusion also to be a kind of deception in that, while it does not defeat the status of "art," it adds little to aesthetic value. Therefore, the preferred status given to painting in this division is not based on its illusionistic capacity, but on the power and probity of formal delineation.[18]

The third division, the art of "sensation," subdivides into the arts of "music" and "color." Color, here, has no relation to painting and, in fact, seems not to refer to any established artform. Kant uses it, evidently, to establish a visual analogue to the auditory "play of sensations" through which he identifies music. Such an analogue imparts a temporal dimension to color perception, a "scanning" of an indefinite field that would require a concept of form different from the spatially delineative one provided by painting. Kant treats music with considerable ambivalence. On the one hand, he places it just below poetry in his hierarchy of value because of its ability to energize the associative powers of cognition "in general," that is, without the limiting intrusions of specific content or illusion. On the other hand, he is not convinced of the inherent rigor of musical form, of its ability to withstand fragmenting into "mere" sensation—thereby tempting appreciation to dissolve into "mere" gratification. In this latter guise, music is demoted to the lowest rank, a judgment that was perhaps reinforced by Kant's personal irritation at music's tendency toward "intrusiveness" into personal privacy.[19]

Kant's division of the arts indicates his curiosity about

art as a symbolic, hence philosophically useful, realm, but it also indicates his considerable indifference to matters of art history or criticism. This very indifference, however, keeps his remarks at a level of generality that proves generative for later interpretations. His ranking of the arts, with poetry at the highest level and architecture at the lowest, undoubtedly influenced Hegel, who adapts this ranking to his own purposes (see Chapter Three). Conversely, Kant's downgrading of architecture through the "form-function" dichotomy, the disjunction between arts and crafts, can be seen as just that "beaux arts" conceit that certain modernist theories, for example, those of the Bauhaus, strove to overthrow. On the other hand, his inclusion of gardening, the decoration of interiors, women's fashions, et cetera, in his discussion of the "language" of painting, presages contemporary impatience with fixed aesthetic categories. In another prescient move, Kant emphasizes the cognitive role of art through his thesis that imagination strengthens the form—not the content—of understanding. This emphasis on form, with its downplaying of narrative and decorative elements, provides the basis for what we know as "formalist aesthetics." Kant's parallel presumption for appreciation, that the peripheral enticements of artworks must be bypassed in the scrutiny of form, is the source for artistic ideologies that seek to eliminate the rewards of enticement from the values they assign to the aesthetic. I return to these issues in the later chapters.

4. APPRECIATION AND CREATIVITY

However much Kant's analysis of art has influenced later theory and practice, in his own system art remains secondary to nature as a source and subject for philosophical reflection. There are some evident extrasystematic reasons for Kant's preferential emphasis from which one can gain some historical perspective. Artworks, particularly in Kant's day, had many didactic and service aspects. They provided lessons in behavior, belief, and the histories of family and empire. They also provided accompaniments for praying, dancing, and dining; and one's familiarity with the subtleties of these functions was usually a reliable indicator of one's social position. Kant's much noted remark about esteeming those individuals who stroll contemplatively in the natural countryside above those who remain at home with their art collections indicates that he was quite aware of these nonaesthetic—even, morally questionable—functions of artworks.[20] A look at the practice of "connoisseurship," a practice that Kant, in contrast to Hegel, did not esteem, can clarify some of these distinctions between the appreciations of nature and art. If aesthetic judgment and the commodification of value are joined in the appreciation of artworks, Kant's thesis of disinterestedness could be extended to hold that artistic connoisseurship can be inhibitory to proper appreciation. Further, when connoisseurs ally their tastes with their prudential interests, their judgments are not of the kind that properly demands universal agreement. Still further, because connoisseurship habituates one to judgments that are vested in interest, it inhibits the free exercise of taste; and if one takes taste as a paradigm for moral judgment, then one can hold that connoisseurship similarly inhibits moral capacity or, at the least, does not support it—which support is the philosophical role that Kant assigns to aesthetic judgment.

This philosophical weakening of appreciation by the encroachment of connoisseurship gives us reason to look further at the aesthetic function that provides us with artworks—the function of creativity. If the desiderata of appreciation are only uneasily sustained by art, what is to be said of creativity—the impulse behind the production of artworks? It is important to note that Kant does not discuss artistic creation in the "Analytic of the Beautiful"; he saves this for the "Analytic of the Sublime." Through this sequestering, he identifies appreciation with the former and creativity with the latter. Kant's account of art making is also more informal than his analysis of appreciation: He makes little attempt to bring creativity under categorical scrutiny and he makes somewhat uncharacteristic use of metaphor. This could suggest that he sees creativity as lacking the rational dimension of appreciation. Artists are characterized as "voices of nature" and, in that capacity, are given the honorific label of "genius," thus indicating that creativity, unlike appreciation, is not open to everyone. The fact of artistic creativity, who is a genius and who is not, is accounted for as a "gift" from nature, one that, in some mysterious way, is bestowed on a chosen few.[21] The process of creativity, how genius makes art, also resists analysis, for it is of the kind that provides no rules upon which future efforts can be based. Kant maintains that the workings of genius cannot be analyzed in the expectation that they might divulge methods for others to emulate: To the contrary, all true geniuses formulate their own rules. As emulation must degenerate into imitation, lesser artists are doomed, it would seem, to—at least, philosophical—failure. It would further seem, given such apparent predetermination, that if artistic activity is thought of as the *aspiration* to genius, it has little to recommend it as a general vocation except for its collective necessity—as in all games of chance, the number of participants enriches the prize. Making art, unlike its appreciation, is not for everyone, and the *effort* at making it, the creative act, is not itself exemplary. Here, Kant does not anticipate the later theories that conceive of artistic activity either as a symptom of social alienation or as a propaedeutic for emotional soundness; and he nowhere suggests that the artistic vocation provides us with a model for moral behavior. Perhaps most important to the distinction he makes between appreciation and creativity, Kant does not indicate, as he does in his moral theory, that it is the "good will"—the intent behind the act rather than its success—that is of primary value: The aesthetic status of genius is consequent on the achieved masterwork; we must first judge the work to find the genius. In contrast, the exercise of taste, like moral action, finds value in the attempt.

I suggest that the reasons behind all this are not only historical but structural. In the brief passages where Kant discusses artistic creativity, a certain characterization emerges: (*a*) Because the abilities of genius are a "gift," the artist lacks responsibility for his success or failure. (*b*) The requirement that the works of genius be "novel" provides the artist with a certain immunity from the norms and rules that others are bound by. Taken together, these characterizations seem not to require that the artist have a moral sensibility. Indeed, they suggest that there is some antagonism between the creative and moral. One can approach this antagonism in another way, and perhaps better understand it, by comparing Kant's construals of beauty and sublimity in nature.

5. SUBLIMITY AND GENIUS

Nature, in Kant's aesthetics, has two faces; one is open and scrutable, the other hidden and rejective. The one corresponds to the subject upon which the analysis of beauty is based; the other face is the subject of the analysis of sublimity. The contrast between them sharpens when we note that Kant allies the appreciation of beauty with "understanding," the faculty for empirical cognition described in the first *Critique,* and that he allies sublimity with "reason," the faculty for moral judgment described in the second *Critique.*[22] I discuss these alliances in turn.

What beauty and empirical knowledge have in common is their basis in sense-data, although, unlike factual claims, the claim that something is beautiful cannot be verified. Imagination is the instrument through which beauty is experienced; and imagination, like understanding, is the mind engaging and structuring sense-data. Unlike understanding, however, imagination does so in the mode of "free play."[23] Now, this is a somewhat peculiar term. Offhand, it would seem that, for Kant, "freedom" is too serious a value to be easily joined with the hedonism of "play"—at least if this joining were meant to support a philosophical claim. Freedom is the governing principle of Kant's moral theory, and he takes pains to distinguish it from mere capriciousness. In the moral sphere, freedom generates choices that deny, or are at least indifferent to, inclination. Play, to the contrary, is one way in which inclination is gratified—through the substitution of fantasy for the more elusive objects of desire. The coupling of "free" and "play," then, might be seen as a restricting of each term by the other, and it is this restriction that leads to Kant's meaning. When play is free, it is not personal; its aim is enjoyment, to be sure, but of a kind that belongs to sensibility "in general," an enjoyment we *all* ought to experience—whatever our separate inclinations.

The mutual restriction that characterizes and makes possible this combination of freedom and play is also, as I claim, the one that grounds the experience of beauty. In my discussion above of Kant's conditions for natural beauty, the valued quality is found in a mediation of extremes, by resolving the incompatibilities of design and freedom. In the present context, value is found in the mediation between two kinds of pleasure—the cognitive pleasure of freedom and the sensual pleasure of play. This mediation provides us with the experience of beauty, and it is brought about by denying aesthetic pleasure the excesses of hedonism, but also by protecting it from the rigidities of preestablished rules. Kant applies the term "beautiful" to those of nature's images that are well formed, harmonious, and complete, and he thus provides imagination the subject within which it is free to play. This is essentially the neoclassic ideal where freedom is generated precisely through its benevolent restriction. Note, however, that the characteristics of "well-formedness, harmony, and completeness" do not constitute an empirical description. Kant makes no claim that certain aspects of nature can be determined to be that way, only that certain of nature's appearances provoke a particular type of experience in us. This is the experience of beauty, and it provides the central philosophical claim of aesthetic judgment, namely, that nature so unified is rational.

But beauty (and its consequences) is not the whole of Kant's concern with nature. He also views nature under another guise, that of "sublimity," and it is here that he explicates another function of the reflective judgment. To experience nature as sublime is to experience it as distorted, chaotic, and fragmented—the negation of the classical ideal of beauty. Yet, sublimity is not simply a series of negations: Its manifestations have their own characteristics, specifically, magnitude and force of a kind that overwhelms the ordering impulse and prohibits both formal unity in the subject and its epistemic containment in an image. Kant's famous examples of the natural sublime are "mountain tops rearing themselves to heaven, deep chasms and streams raging therein, deep shadowed solitudes that dispose one to melancholy meditations."[24] The experience of sublimity in nature cannot be subsumed under appreciation, for it exceeds the capacities of disinterested perception and, instead, impinges, often with a threat of danger, on the perceiver. But such experience does evoke a certain response: awe, fear, and a desire to withdraw. Kant characterizes this as a withdrawal of the mind into itself, the mind's "self-affirmation" through reason of its capacity to produce an idea of that which cannot be contained or unified by sensory perception—that which appears to defy the laws of nature. He states: "The sublime . . . is an object [of nature] the representation of which determines the mind to think the unattainability of nature regarded as a presentation of ideas."[25]

The appreciation of beauty serves as a model of moral disposition because the subjective lawlikeness of its process invokes, and thereby supports, the law upon which moral duty is based. The results of creativity, works of art, indicate that the efforts of genius, inscrutable as they are, invariably result in the formal order of beauty, an order that points to the rationality of empirical nature, that is, its uniformity and predictability. The creative *act*, however, is not like either of these: Its outcome is not predictable, nor can its workings be subsumed under any law. In this sense, creativity can be considered the human counterpart of the natural sublime: It cannot be accounted for through a concept of experience—of the "understanding"—but, like its natural counterpart, it can be encompassed by an idea. This is the idea of infinite force and magnitude, which is an idea of reason; and our capacity to hold such an idea identifies sublimity as also a symbol of morality. But sublimity does not present morality as the equilibrium between a law that is self-given and its demand of the self for unconditional obedience—that is the provenance of beauty. Instead, sublimity can be seen to symbolize morality in a different way: as the rational idea of an infinite task and, hence, as an imperative directed at the achievement of this task.[26] The Kantian ideal of the moral perfectibility of humankind is one such task. I suggest here that the striving for fulfillment of the creative impulse is another. In Chapter Three I show that these ideals of sublimity anticipate the Hegelian thesis of progress in art and culture.

Kant's description of artistic creativity is in the Platonic mode of the "possessed poet": Artists are instruments and voices of a higher wisdom to which they have access but do not themselves understand; they are inspired "naifs"—indifferent to the basis of their actions and, thus, not answerable for these actions.[27] Creativity so construed is the converse of appreciation; it provides no model for emulation by another individual and no insights into the formation of attitudes or dispositions that might be worthy of esteem. The artist, like the storm at sea, is best experienced at a distance. With the forces of sublimity one has every right to be prudent—an attitude that contrasts with the "disinterestedness" called for by the images of beauty. It is not that Kant construes the artist as "immoral," for this would entail a puritanical association of creativity with evil that, in general, is quite foreign to him. Rather, Kant gives the artist a "natural" morality, one that is more like that of beasts than humans: A beast has no alternative to characteristic action and thus cannot be "blamed" for any particular action, and the "nobility" we find in certain animals is also not of their making. Such a natural morality does not devolve from a "good will." Rather, it is the issue of an exclusive innocence and transparency that is, in fact, the common and necessary form of the activities of genius. We cannot make this form determinate, any more than we can determine the form of beauty. It would seem, then, after all distinctions have been invoked, the characteristics of genius have this compatibility with the characteristics of beautiful art: They can only be understood through reflection. Kant's philosophical claims for art are thus justified in two ways: The images of art can be traced to their sources in natural beauty, and the origins of artworks can be traced to their origins in the natural sublime—to the artist as "nature's voice."

6. LATER THEORY

One consequence of this construal of creativity, of Kant's exempting the artist qua artist from conventional demands of moral responsibility, is the expanded role it plays in later aesthetic theory. I suggest here that in this theoretical alliance of the artist with the natural sublime lies the common beginning of two later, often conflicting views of artistic activity. One is found in the identification of artists with eccentricity and marginality; the other enshrines the artist as a seer and prophet. I take these in turn.

One historical path leads from genius to the artist as "bohemian" and "neurotic"; here, creative ability becomes equated with civil disobedience and mental illness. This thesis is developed in Schopenhauer, is given extended expression in Freudian theory, and becomes a commonplace in both serious and popular writings on modern art. In Schopenhauer, the artist is distinguished from the "ordinary" individual through the ability to trace nature through its conventional representations to its underlying principle—"will." In the later versions, the tracings of creativity are directed to the will's historical successor—to the subconscious realm of impulse and desire over which rationality has no sway.

In the writings of Hegel resides the other theme: the artist as world-historical individual, one whose visionary efforts project themselves through public symbols of culture's "progress" rather than through revelations of a noumenal "inner nature." Hegel's artists differ from

Schopenhauer's in that they have little concern with, rather than little control over, personal or prudential matters. Great art, in this context, furnishes appreciation with a historically prescient image that in troubled times, as in modernism, becomes a socially critical image. For Hegel, art functions to both document and define the directed course—the teleology—of historical change.

TWO

Schopenhauer

1. COMPARISON WITH KANT

NEOCLASSICISTS of the Enlightenment might view the manifestations of sublimity as merely surface disorders of the deeper harmony of beauty—as symptomatic of the imperfect world with which, ideally, art ought not to be concerned. Competing Romantics would argue that the sublime is actually beauty's antithetical principle and that its "disorders" are signs, for those willing to look, of a reality that is masked by the conventions and artifices of social institutions. In Kant's theory, artistic genius is identified with the capacity to probe that conventional surface and produce images of what lies beyond it. The reality suggested by these images—the noumenal world—Kant supposes to be both rational and benign. Indeed, this supposition forms the basis of his hopes for the expansion of knowledge and a just world. Given this hope, Kant would not consider that the artistic revelations of this world, either in appreciation or creativity, could have a negative subject.

In the philosophy of Arthur Schopenhauer one finds a very different picture.[1] The Kantian image of noumenal reality is transformed—better, inverted—into a principle that is both irrational and destructive: Schopenhauer's noumenon is "will," and its workings underlie both the processes of the natural world and our psychic life. Kant provides us with an architectonic image of order and completeness; Schopenhauer's image is one of flux and chaos. Although the workings of the will have no point or goal, its manifestations in the world of our conventional, scientific and ethical, representations are such as to deceive us about the aimlessness of its processes. Equally, its manifestations in our lives, our ambitions and desires, disguise the essential "meaninglessness" of our existence. In Schopenhauer's theory, the artist is one of the epistemic instruments through which the deceptions of the will are exposed; and the appreciation of art provides the insights through which these deceptions can be bypassed. One consequence of this revelatory capacity of art is the price that it exacts from the artist: The act of creation, given the nature of its subject, is also an act of self-immolation. The artistic quest is destructive to the artist.

2. THE NOUMENAL WILL

Schopenhauer's construal of the artist is of particular historical significance. It is an early version of the many later theories that associate a panoply of social and psychological afflictions with creativity: the artist's alienation from self and others, the neurotic fears and the realities of rejection, and other forms of psychosocial instability. These afflictions can be regarded as internal consequences of the artistic vocation, and equally as manifestations of social animosity towards the artist. Accordingly, Schopenhauer's thesis can also be taken as an early warning of the later, Romantic and modern, antagonisms between art and society. The appreciation of art, as well as its creation, is given an antisocial cast by Schopenhauer: Through the "truths" that artworks present, we come to know the noumenal will in a way that runs counter to its conventional representations. Great art does not present the world through the particularities of individual things, for such things are merely the phenomenal manifestations of process of the will. Rather, artworks image things as they would be if free of the distortions of process: things as "essences." The power of art lies in its ability to present phenomenal images of noumenal reality, for Schopenhauer equates these essences with his version of the Kantian thing-in-itself. Artistic creativity bypasses the conventionalized representations of the world—representations that are offered as empirical and moral laws—in order to provide insights about the will's essential nature. The adequate appreciation of art is tantamount to gaining knowledge of the world these insights reveal, and this gives art its epistemic dimension. But Schopenhauer goes further; he also gives art a moral function: Our coming to know the will "as it is in itself" enables us to escape its demands—its "ravages"—and, thus, enables us to regain our individual moral dignity. We escape the irrational insistence of willed action by inaction, a withdrawal into the peace of contemplation.[2]

Kant's view of the relationship between knowledge and the noumenal world is, of course, very different. Even in his most speculative moments, Kant does not indicate that we can know the noumenon, only that we can infer its necessity for the completeness of knowledge. This inference is made on primarily rational grounds, but Kant does reach back to the phenomenal evidence of the reflective judgment for its support: This judgment identifies something in nature that facilitates reflection. It is not simply a matter of thinking, however, of concluding for theoretical purposes that nature must be (taken as) rational. Nature, properly viewed, looks that way—although reflection does not tell us why—and art, when at its best, follows nature in presenting images of order and harmony. Accordingly, Kant refers this judgment of beauty in art and nature to sensibility and calls it "aesthetic."

Although Schopenhauer follows Kant in searching for a

way to transcend the skeptical impasse between the world as perceived and the world as it is, he does not have Kant's scruples about the limitations of knowledge. The epistemic capacity that Schopenhauer ascribes to art gives it full metaphysical access to the "world as will." Artworks represent the noumenal world as it really is—not as we hope it is. By proposing that a world to which our empirical representations do not refer is actually knowable, Schopenhauer rejects the critical limitations that Kant places on philosophy. Although the ontological division between the world as "will" and as "representation" gives Schopenhauer's system a nominally dualistic cast, he overcomes this by adopting (although he would have denied it) the Hegelian strategy of rejecting the dualism by fiat. His ontological unity is achieved by dividing knowledge rather than the world. Schopenhauer's claim is that noumenal knowledge is of a different and philosophically higher order than knowledge of phenomena. He accounts for empirical knowledge through his "principle of sufficient reason," which is essentially an analysis of material causality. His analysis of noumenal knowledge, on the other hand, is grounded in the contemplative epistemologies of Indian philosophy.[3] Hegel, in his famous polemic against Kant's epistemic limitation on noumenal reality, argues that because we cannot posit existence for something we cannot know, reality—in reality—is a "fusion" of thought and the world (see Chapter Three). Schopenhauer does not go this far, however, and he maintains the distinction between inner and outer by assigning his divided knowledge to different locations: While the will as it is objectified in nature can be known through causal analysis of the external world, it is most immediately and directly experienced in our affective life, through our internal awareness of our own feelings. This separation of knowledge into external and internal, "objective" and "subjective," further distinguishes Schopenhauer from Kant, who largely excludes the emotions from rationality; and it also distinguishes him from Hegel, who posits the absorption of the emotions within rationality.

3. NATURE AS PROCESS

Schopenhauer finds phenomenal evidence for noumenal reality in the processes of change that underlie the extensional surface of the world. When taken formally, these processes—the incessant building and tearing down of nature's hierarchies—can be recognized as the ongoing strivings of the will. As content, the differentiations achieved through these processes—the gradations from geologic forms through animate life to sentience—echo another of the will's manifestations: the development of human cultural history. The patterns of change that are evidenced in geologic formations and biological species are continuous with the edifices we erect and destroy in the course of history. At the one end of this continuum we speak of "natural processes," and at the other, of "desires and ambitions." The first is the language of empirical description; the second is the language of self-consciousness; for Schopenhauer, the principle is the same.

The much-noted "pessimism" of Schopenhauer is in his rejection of the thesis that the processes of both nature and human culture can be accounted for teleologically, through the posit of an end or goal. For him, the evolution of natural forms has no direction; it is not guided by an intrinsic rationality or by a divine plan seeking fulfillment. Equally, the attempts we make to fulfill our lives through ideals based on generational continuity are essentially random gestures, as devoid of meaning as are the patterns of change in nature.[4] This rejection of teleology identifies a fundamental contrast between the theories of

Schopenhauer and Hegel, but it also, in a lesser respect, contrasts with Kant's views on the matter. Hegel considers all events and processes to be guided by a rationality that is both immanent and transcendent, that provides both mechanism and goal. Kant, more circumspectly, gives the premise of teleology the stature of a reflective judgment, regulatory for thought if not demonstrable in fact.[5] Of the three philosophers under discussion here, Schopenhauer is alone in totally rejecting the notion of a divinity to which the design of nature and existential meaning can be imputed and thereby demonstrated. In this, Schopenhauer differs most completely from Hegel, for whom the entire course of the world, the "evolution of spirit," is directed toward an ultimate eschatological reunion with God. With Kant, the existence of God remains a purely speculative idea; nevertheless, the authenticity of his moral imperative requires, at least, an ideal of divinity, because through such an ideal, morality is saved from the accusation of arbitrariness. In this respect, Kant's strong distinction between knowledge and speculation—a distinction that is glossed over by both the others—makes noumenal knowledge, whether of God or of the world behind appearances, a thesis that is at the same time practically essential and systematically unprovable.

Actually, the philosophical consequence of Schopenhauer's metaphysical position is not skepticism, as is often assumed. For him there is no problem with knowing the world, as there would be for the skeptic; the problem, rather, is with finding a good reason to live in the world. Schopenhauer's solution can better be characterized as a form of stoicism in which he couples the possibility of a "will-less," hence nonempirical knowledge with an important consequence of such knowledge: Given the way the world really is, the proper stance toward living in it must be a refusal to act according to the dictates of the will.

Schopenhauer takes pains to distinguish this will-less form of knowledge from empirical representations, the scientific theories that provide factual knowledge. He also distinguishes it from the legal and political representations that provide rules and norms for social behavior. In Schopenhauer's view, the claims of objectivity and neutrality attributed to any such representations are actually self-serving, for it is in the nature of the will's striving to be (self) deceptive, to conceal its pointlessness in our purposes. Consequently, we cannot ascertain from representations that are complicitous with such deception what our moral response to the world should be.

All this is, indeed, oppressive and depressing, and a theory that ends here would have little claim on our continued attention. But Schopenhauer does identify a form of knowledge that can transcend this negativity and, thereby, provide us with a propaedeutic for the moral life: the knowledge conveyed by the images of art. I approach this issue as I do with Kant—through Schopenhauer's views on the contrasts between beauty and sublimity. Schopenhauer follows Kant by situating the appreciation and creation of art in the tension between these values, but his approach is quite different.

4. BEAUTY AND SUBLIMITY

The shift in aesthetic emphasis from appreciation to creativity that occurred between the eighteenth and nineteenth centuries coincides with the shift in attention from the beautiful in nature to nature as sublime.[6] I take this parallelism, not as mere coincidence, but as a reciprocal influence between theories—and I use it here as a way of interpreting the transition from Kant to Schopenhauer. When we follow Kant and take beauty as the central aesthetic value, we refer to the characteristics of both its object and its appreciation, and we mean on the one side the formal ordering of parts and on the other the special view we take of the ordered whole. The overall distinction between these, between the qualities of form and the mode of perception, is essential to the aesthetic judgment; and when, as with Kant, we attribute "purposiveness" to the former and "disinterestedness" to the latter, other distinctions are also implied. The object as the subject of beauty is distinct from its conventional identity: It is both less and more—both "mere" form and "pure" form. It is also distinct from the history of its origins, whether natural or human: It is beautiful only in its completeness and its immediacy; it is a thing that exists fully in the eternal present. The appreciation of beauty also requires a distinction, a separation of the aesthetic self from the conventional self: We must be dispassionate toward our object and indifferent to our own inclinations, allowing ourselves only the satisfaction attendant on replacing the useful facts of practical existence with the useless value of selfless contemplation. For such "uselessness" to be an aesthetic virtue, we must regard our own history and the history of our subject, as disruptive to proper appreciation—although we know that both the circumstances of our past and the origins of our subject foster the accomplishment of appreciation.

Beauty, in this sense, is a thing of balanced distinctions, from which excess and paucity in both form and attitude are excluded. A central difference between beauty and sublimity is that sublimity denies this balance and embraces excess—even at the risk of ending with paucity. First thought of as a flaw that occurs when beauty is extended into the more unruly aspects of nature and sensibility, sublimity soon becomes beauty's theoretical contrary and historical competitor. For Kant and the Enlightenment, sublimity in nature is not a subject for appreciation; it does not provide models for either deportment or art. Sensibility, according to Kant, moves away from sublimity to the refuge of reason, in which unlimited vastness and power are important only as ideas. With the rise of Romanticism, however, the natural sublime does become a model for both deportment and art, and the values that characterize both the form of beauty and its appreciation are undermined. Chaos, immensity, and boundlessness replace harmony, moderation, and clarity as values in both art and life. The ensuing disorder itself becomes a value. Kant's thesis that art emulates the beauties of nature is replaced by the new sentiment that artistic creativity emulates the *processes* of nature: Excess is no longer an aberration subject to the control of reason; it is the pathway to the appreciation of a nature that is valued precisely for its own excesses. The emulation of sublimity in aesthetic experience replaces the Kantian dispassionate stance and narrows the distance between agent and subject. Artwork and appreciation come together within a framework that emphasizes movement rather than architectonics—the dynamics of process over the stabilities of form—and the neoclassic vices of distortion, ambiguity, dissonance, become the virtues of Romanticism.[7]

The metaphors that are used above to characterize sublimity also seem to provide fitting images for Schopenhauer's principle of the will. What, after all, could be more romantic than a metaphysics that stresses the insatiable and the irrational? But characterizing Schopenhauer's theories only in this way would be misleading, if not entirely mistaken. I do believe that Schopenhauer's evocation of the will did much to stir the Romantic imagination, but he also gives artistic creativity and moral life a tragic and quietistic dimension that belies those later enthusiasms and theatricalities. To my mind, it is more accurate to consider Schopenhauer as a bridge between the Enlightenment and Romanticism—as providing the latter with a variety of themes and insights, while still remaining obsessed with the crumbling ideals of the former. This can be shown through a closer look at his treatments of the will and sublimity.

Although Schopenhauer does characterize the will in the romantic metaphors of the sublime, he advises that we can, and must, withdraw from the world it creates. Through the assumed posture of passivity and quietude, we can then negate its influence on us. This posture is not, however, to be equated with the "disinterestedness" that is Kant's propaedeutic for both the experience of beauty and moral judgment. It is, in effect, Kant's thesis gone sour—disbelieved but not supplanted. Because Schopenhauer views the world through the oppressive metaphors of the sublime rather than the conciliatory ones of beauty, he also rejects Kant's proposal that beauty provides the phenomenal basis for justifying morality as engaged action *within* the world.[8] The question, then, is what form of experience provides the basis for Schopenhauer's alternative—his morality of disengagement.

For Schopenhauer, the differences between the experiences of beauty and sublimity can be found in the ways phenomena, the different "objectifications" of the will, relate to another of the will's objectifications: our own bodies. The experience of beauty involves an accommodation between the object and our experiences that requires the Kantian juncture of "purposiveness" and "disinterestedness." Beauty poses no threat to us; it merely asks that we suspend our own willing in its appreciation. It thus provides us with the valuable illusion of a reciprocal harmony between nature and ourselves. Sublimity breaks this illusion through progressive stages of discord. Will that is manifest in nature's cataclysms is a threat to the will of our own being—our interest in self-preservation.

However, the appreciation of sublimity, experiencing danger as sublime, involves a "sublimation" of fear by shifting the locus of the experience from our vulnerability to our indifference. Fear is transformed into will-less contemplation: The threat is universalized; and the subject, stripped of its menace, is revealed as essence.[9]

The "universality" through which Schopenhauer brings the sublime into appreciation is more charged than the one Kant requires for the appreciation of beauty; it is achieved in the face of—by pushing aside—a compelling interest of our will. Experiencing sublimity is a heroism of self-abnegation to which Schopenhauer finds a counterpart in the meditative practices of Indian religions.[10] But it is also a heroism of the exalted self: a self-given challenge to go beyond the limits of reason and reasonableness.[11] These limits are found not only in the physical dangers of the natural sublime but in the conventional boundaries of what is acceptable as normal behavior and social order. The transgression of these boundaries, together with the risks this entails, furnishes us with the popular image of antisocial bohemianism. But Schopenhauer finds no theatrics in such transgressions; for him, their purpose is epistemic: To open oneself to those aspects of the world that are collectively feared and avoided is to defeat the hold that the will has on our knowing. Here, one could take Schopenhauer to mean that all true knowledge is a coming to terms with what is feared and avoided, for the world thus revealed provides us with the moral alternative to the world of our willing. To be moral in Schopenhauer's sense entails withdrawal, and the risk is anonymity and loneliness. Perhaps the loneliness of morality is the last and greatest of sublimity's dangers that must be embraced.

While knowledge of the essential world is propaedeutic to personal morality, its symbolization is the function of art. It is here that the particular ambiguity of the artistic vocation shows itself: The symbolic presentation of the world as essence involves action *within* the world of the will. Schopenhauer does not permit artists the philosophical luxury of withdrawal into moral "wholeness"; he keeps their selves divided—between the act of creating and its social consequences. Schopenhauer's pessimism reasserts itself here: Just as there is no expectation that the revelations of art will accrue to the general good, there is little chance that creativity will be rewarded. While this thesis does not undermine the epistemic importance of art, it does suggest that artistic creativity, divided as it is between action and content, can only to be reconciled in the asceticism of the contemplative—philosophical—stance. Such reconciliation, of course, would be at the expense of action, and it would thus deny the continuing tradition of art. Here we find an echo of Hegel, who also sees art's reliance on the sensual as a limitation on its philosophical role.

5. ART AND THE PLATONIC IDEA

Schopenhauer considers the images of the world that artworks present to be free of the distortions that other representations, those in the service of the will, are prone to. In his attempt to show precisely what it is about the representations of art that gives them this freedom, Schopenhauer reaches back to the Platonic "idea"—the theory of Forms through which Plato famously distinguishes between the pheonomenal world of particulars and the conceptual world of essences. Schopenhauer puts the matter thus: "If, therefore, the object has . . . passed out of all relation to something outside it, and the subject has passed out of all relation to the will, what is known is no longer the individual thing as such, but the Idea, the eternal form."[12]

Despite this acknowledgment of the earlier theory, Schopenhauer's use of the form-thing relationship in his aesthetics is quite different from Plato's. Plato distinguishes between Forms and things in the sense that the latter are intelligible through their "participation" in the former. This participation identifies separate things as sharing a common characteristic and thus deserving a common name; it also identifies individual things as having incidental characteristics that do not contribute to their collective identity. Forms, to the contrary, in that they are pure essences, have nothing superfluous, and are thus more real than the things organized and categorized through them. To use a famous example: The "form of bed" is more real than the many beds that are its instantiations. For Plato, the incidental diversities that distinguish between separate beds are not virtues; they are hindrances to conceptual clarity—to the precision with which we organize the world into arrays of formal instantiations. Plato regards art as a particularly insidious hindrance in that its representations cloud things that are already unclear. He also regards this obfuscation as willful: The world as a (natural) jumble of imperfect instantiations is bad enough; art's imitations further distort these imperfections through the subjective whims and caprices of artists. It follows from this that art, construed as a distortion of imperfections, is at a third remove from the true reality presented by the Forms. As the quest for truth is one of Plato's highest virtues, it also follows that his characterization of art as distortive turns into the accusation that it is deceptive. Here we have the basis for Plato's deep suspicion of art's social role, and his famous enjoinder that the efforts of artists should be subject to social control. Plato's argument is well known: True knowledge is desirable and can be attained through rational thought; the images of art are a hindrance to this effort; and therefore, art should be restricted. To this might be added that, as philosopher-statesmen (ideally) exhibit the highest degree of rationality, it is their task—through specifications of form and theme, and through censorship—to regulate works of art.[13]

Schopenhauer reverses the terms of this argument and comes to an entirely different conclusion. For him, it is in the representations of art that the essences of the world are revealed. Far from being obfuscatory, art presents things as they truly are, free from the distortions of the will, and it is in the special nature of the creative process, the artist's "vision," that this adequacy of representation is found. Plato, within his scheme of social stratification, regards artists as (mere) artisans largely incapable of philosophical understanding. Kant gives artists a more elevated role in the philosophical enterprise, for he has them function as oracular voices that invoke a compatibility between nature as it is and as it is perceived. But Kant does not analyze the dynamics of these voices, the nature of the artistic process, and he directs the understanding of their message to appreciation. Schopenhauer, in contrast, does attempt such an analysis, and he redirects an important share of philosophical understanding to creativity.

Schopenhauer's will can be compared to Plato's Forms in the sense that both function as the underlying principles of their respective cosmologies. Plato's is a principle of rationality, of order and stability; Schopenhauer's is a principle of process and change that is indifferent to rationality. Plato's principle is to be sought out and emulated; Schopenhauer's is to be overcome and rejected. Plato's is the source of the "good"; Schopenhauer's, the ground of deception and, hence, of evil. To complete this inversion: For Plato, art is an instrument that distorts reality and propogates falsehood, while Schopenhauer sees art's penetration through the illusory world of will's creations as revelatory.

Curiously, however, it is the Platonic world of Forms that Schopenhauer has his artist discover, and this tension—between Forms and will—is destabilizing to his ontology. Will is Schopenhauer's noumenon, and the world consists of its objectifications. But such objectifications, the representations, for example, of science, are not real in the Platonic sense because they are in the "service" of the will: They are part of the temporal world of continual, purposeless transformation. The artist's vision, to the contrary, presents what Schopenhauer calls "adequate objectifications" of the will. That vision "plucks the object of its contemplation from the stream of the world's course, and holds it isolated before it. This particular thing, which in that stream was an infinitesimal part, becomes for art a representative of the whole, an equivalent of the infinitely many in time and space. . . . it stops the wheel of time."[14] Being a "representative of the whole" is, of course, the relationship Plato's Forms have to their instances, and thus, one can see why Schopenhauer has his artworks image things as Forms. But where Plato's ontology is neatly divided between the worlds of Forms and things, of which the former is more "real" than the latter, Schopenhauer's ontology has three members: will, things, and Forms. The first, will, is the noumenon—the "thing-in-itself." The second, "things in the world," is complicit with the first by virtue of misrepresenting it. The third, "Forms," is adequate to the first when representing the second as it would be when free of the first. This is an unbalanced idealism, flawed perhaps by playing the contrasting notions of "essence" and "process" against each other without assigning primacy to either. However, while such indecision about ontological first principles may indeed be systematically damaging, it supports my construal of Schopenhauer as a bridge between (opposing principles of) the Enlightenment and Romanticism. Further, his elevation of "process" to such ontological contention, coupled with his insistance on art's epistemic capacity, provides aesthetics with a new focus: the nature of creativity.

6. ARTISTIC CREATIVITY

Although Schopenhauer differs from Plato by giving artists access to noumenal knowledge, the road to this ideal world is not very different in either theory. In Plato's version, as described in the *Phaedrus*, the chariot of the soul is pulled by the mismatched horses of emotion and rationality. The struggle between appetite and duty being unequal, the immediate pleasures of wayside grazing thwart the soul's quest for knowledge and doom it to repeating the effort in later incarnations. The chariots of the gods, on the other hand, are equipped with better matched steeds; and by virtue of this symmetry, the gods, in coursing around the rim of the heavens, are provided with a glimpse of the unmediated Forms—thus succeeding where humans fail.

It seems, then, that Plato's gods and Schopenhauer's artists are alike, and both different from "ordinary" humans, in this one respect: They both have access to a world undistorted by particularity and desire. But the similarity quickly ends. The gods, on their part, seem content with the knowledge they have gained, for it strengthens them in their status, in the "godliness" of their behavior and, practically, in their function as role models for humankind. In contrast, Schopenhauer's artists fare quite poorly, for although creative activity provides access to the reality behind appearances, the effort to reach and present this reality through the images of art is destructive to those who make it. In Schopenhauer's aesthetic, the role of the artist does not provide a model for emulation—only the artwork does. However, since Schopenhauer does include artistic creativity within his epistemology, the dilemma he presents the artist is that creative work is inevitably at odds with what becomes known through it, namely, that work is futile. Even as artists come to understand what their efforts reveal, they seem compelled to continue these efforts, and thus, they remain caught within a world they should know to reject. This thesis, that artists are unable to heed the implications of the knowledge revealed to them by their own creations is, as I believe, at the source of Schopenhauer's provocative correlation of artistic creativity with social and psychological maladjustment. This dilemma of creativity is not, in itself, a philosophical value for Schopenhauer; it is merely the price that one such value—access to the will—extracts. The identification of artistic creativity *as* a value is not to be directly found in Schopenhauer; this belongs to a later time, to Romanticism and the aesthetics of expression. It is my contention, however, that Schopenhauer's extended analysis of the artistic process provides a major impetus for such theories. I discuss this further in Chapter Five.

If Kant's artist is nature's voice, Schopenhauer's artist becomes its victim. This shift in characterization comes about through Schopenhauer's answer to a question asked by him but not by Kant: What are the consequences for the artist of being "nature's voice"? The specifics of this answer are actually quite familiar to us as they are all versions of the modernist fascination with creativity as a self-revelatory process. Here, artistic creativity provides a clearer, if more corrosive, insight into self and world than the rest of us dare or are capable of having. Philosophers and mystics are also, perhaps more consistently, capable of such insights; but artists remain positioned between private insight and the public nature of artworks. The consequences of the conflicting demands of revelatory content and social acceptance—accusation seeking praise from the accused—are invariably self-destructive. Schopenhauer posits a particular affinity between creativity and madness, indeed, the "disposition to madness" that marks "every advance of the intellect."[15] He attributes the artistic version of madness to extraordinary focus on the "presentness" of perception and to the concomitant distortion of memory. Memory, being a relational temporal function, provides the usual perspective through which responses become adequate to events. Artistic concentration on immediate response, the recasting of all events, past and present, into a nontemporal "now," weakens this perspective by disregarding the temporal linkage—the causal connections—between events. Insisting on the presentness of experience removes explanation from the available methods through which events can be controlled. As a result, coping with life becomes more difficult, and this gives artists the veneer of eccentricity that, in the extreme case, becomes the substance of madness. Being in the "eternal present," however, is also a characteristic of the essences that are the content of artworks—Forms do not exist in time—and so the self-destructiveness of creativity is also a sign of its adequacy for its subject.

Schopenhauer does not see these consequences of creativity as providing the impetus for a collective catharsis, one in which we are all strengthened and purified by art's revelations. Schopenhauer's pessimism, as I indicate above, entails rejecting the linkage between "progress" and "process." Accordingly, although he considers art to be truth bearing, he does not expect its truths to influence social change; the lessons of art are only for the solitary receptive individual.

As a historical aside, I note that Schopenhauer's works were written during the period when the Enlightenment belief in social rationality was crumbling, and the emerging alternative, Hegelian historicism, had a strongly speculative cast. But rather than accept what he considered the metaphysical excesses of Hegel—the optimistic identification of rationality with historical ascendency—Schopenhauer, on this issue, remained a creature of the old order, preferring the stasis and dignity of failure to the new attempts at justifying action. In this sense, Schopenhauer can be considered an ethical elitist, a latter-day Stoic, for he reserves the possibility of adequate response to the world to just those individuals who can understand the truth about its nature. On this point he states: "When my teaching reaches its highest point, it assumes a *negative* character and so ends up with a negation. Thus it can speak here only of what is denied or given up; but what is gained in place of this, what is laid hold of, it is forced . . . to describe as nothing."[16]

The response this truth suggests is that of self-imposed isolation and withdrawal from the world. But the modalities of isolation, contemplation and the dispassionate gaze, are reserved for the ethically transparent and unified individual. These modalities—they cannot be called actions—are also elitist in the sense that, on the model of appreciation, they require a degree of leisure. Artists, while they provide us with contemplation's objects, do not have that leisure and thus, on this score as well, must inhabit the world their own works disown. Schopenhauer's descriptions of creative life and its consequences are quite sensitive and prescient, but he offers little help. His artist remains a theoretical entity, an instrument through which art makes its unique contribution to the philosophical system. In this sense, Schopenhauer is close to Kant, for the only artist of concern to either is the one capable of providing the content that philosophy requires—the artist as "genius." Inasmuch as Schopenhauer's theory, unlike Kant's, ties creativity to affliction, it implies that genius, because most creative, is also most afflicted. An inversion of this idea, one that gained later popularity, is that the greater the affliction, the higher the level of genius. This inversion moves creativity away from the philosophical role that Schopenhauer ascribes to it—as an epistemic pathway to the realm of "ideas"—into a new identity as "self-expression." I return to this issue in Chapter Five.

7. CLASSIFICATION OF THE ARTS

Given the importance of art to eighteenth- and nineteenth-century philosophical theories, the aesthetic components of these theories, as shown in the preceding chapter on Kant, include taxonomies, or classifications, of art forms. The aim of these classifications is not simply to differentiate the various arts through their formal characteristics but to weigh the relative strength of the contribution each art form makes to the overall system. The historical succession of theories is marked by greater categorical complexity: Schopenhauer's theory is more comprehensive than Kant's, although less so than that of Hegel. Kant's relatively cursory treatment of art forms is in keeping with his belief that, philosophically, art is merely an extension of the aesthetics of nature. Given Schopenhauer's coupling of art with the Platonic idea, his taxonomy of art forms is more systematic: He distinguishes between art forms according to their ability to image, as ideas, the ascending "grades" of the will's instantiations in the world.

Schopenhauer did not seem to rely much on looking, perhaps because he regarded the spatial manifold as the will in its geological—its slowest and most rudimentary—

manifestations. But he listened carefully, and responded to music as neither Kant nor Hegel ever did. Schopenhauer gives music the highest position on his scale of philosophical capability because he regards music, of all the arts, as capable of presenting the will *independently* of its spatial objectifications. The visual arts—painting, sculpture, and even the descriptions of literature—present images, albeit "adequate" ones, of the will's objectifications; they represent the way the will shows itself in the things of the world. Music, however, as it is a nonrepresentational, phenomenally temporal art, goes beyond the function of imaging and presents itself as the formal analogue of the essence of the will itself—as pure process.

Schopenhauer justifies this claim in two ways: through the correspondence he finds between the harmonic structure of music and the taxonomy of natural forms, and through the correspondence between the dynamics of music and the flow of our emotional life—our world of feelings. The first of these provides us with a somewhat quaint cosmology: Using classical harmony as a model, Schopenhauer correlates its four voices with the levels of nature, from the rudimentary beat of geologic change as manifested in the bass voice, through the hierarchies of the plant and animal kingdoms in the tenor and alto voices, culminating in the range of human aspirations voiced through the soprano.

Although Schopenhauer assigns the nonmusical arts a more limited role, their classification proceeds along the same lines: He begins with architecture, "whose aim is to elucidate the will at the lowest level of objectivity," and ends with tragedy in drama, "which presents to us . . . at the highest grade of the will's objectification that very conflict of the will with itself."[17]

Music, however, bypasses the tasks of imaging or describing the will's objectifications, for its reference is to the internal reality of human feelings, and both reference and subject are in the temporal form of process. This referential capacity gives music its unique normative and aesthetic position. Schopenhauer's thesis, here, can be put this way: Our most direct evidence of the will comes not from our knowlege of the "external" world, but through our introspective awareness of our own willing—the dynamics of our emotional life. As the "medium" of this awareness, our feelings, is both internal and temporal, the art closest to it is music, which replicates the form of feelings in its own cadences and progressions. Music, therefore, does not represent the will through imaging; it is, rather, the will's direct analogue. As Schopenhauer puts it, "music differs from all the other arts by the fact that it is not a copy of the phenomenon . . . but is directly a copy of the Will itself, and therefore expresses the metaphysical to everything physical in the world, the thing-in-itself to every phenomenon." And again: "The inexpressible depth of music . . . is due to the fact that it reproduces all the emotions of our innermost being, but entirely without reality and remote from its pain."[18]

The suggestiveness of Schopenhauer's thesis here can be offset by its many difficulties: Musical form is specified, at least in part, by musical notation. But the "form of will" is a metaphysical notion, perhaps a poetic conceit, for which no specification can be given. And the "form of feeling" also defies specification, either because it, too, is a poetic metaphor or because we lack the proper tools. So what does it mean to say that these forms are analogous? How can we show which are—whether they are?[19]

Despite these analytic difficulties, however, Schopenhauer's thesis has accrued a good deal of historical strength. The form-feeling conflation would certainly not have been strange to the early admirers of, say, Berlioz or Mahler or Berg. To them it probably seemed prescient, and it still is part of critical language. As for early psychological attempts to make sense of subconscious processes, the analogy between will, music, and affective life surely provided welcome insights, even if later on, as with much of depth psychology, it lost its authority. As aesthetic and psychological explanations, it may be that "forms of feeling" and the "subconscious" stand or fall together.

8. THE HEGELIAN ALTERNATIVE

In the following chapter, I extend my discussion of the aesthetics of Kant and Schopenhauer to the aesthetics of Hegel. Some preliminary comparisons of the three may prove helpful here. I have shown that Kant's metaphors for the experience of beauty in nature are primarily visual: One walks in the countryside and reflects on the completeness one sees in the dispositions of nature. The breeze on one's cheek and the hum of insects may add to this—but vision is primary. Through this emphasis, Kant brings Descartes's identification of knowledge with the "light of nature" into the rational ideal of "enlightenment."[20] When it comes to art, however, Kant abandons the visual metaphor of knowledge by giving epistemic preference to the least phenomenal art—the discursive art of poetry. This choice is the one Hegel also makes in establishing his heirarchy of the arts. Kant's reason for elevating poetry above the other arts is much like Hegel's, namely, that because poetry is discursive and nonphenomenal, it is closer to the language of rationality—of philosophy. Schopenhauer, to the contrary, through his insistence on the primacy of subjectivity, stands against the other two in the ongoing debate over the priority between thought and feeling. Schopenhauer gives tragedy the highest position among the imaging arts, not because it is discursive, but because it is best able to show the wretchedness of life, when the individual will comes into conflict—as it must—with universal willing. Music rises above this only because its presentation of the will to feeling is unconflicted, without pain. On the other hand, Hegel and Schopenhauer are alike in seeing the world as process; but Hegel's process, unlike Schopenhauer's, is directed: It is process as progress. In the Hegelian scheme, the entire history of art is a symbol of progress, and in its course, the phenomenal arts are superseded by the arts of discourse; thus music gives way to poetry. But the history of progress, for Hegel, extends beyond the history of art, and in this succession, the arts as a whole eventually give way to other—higher—epistemic forms: religion and, ultimately, philosophy.

THREE

Hegel

1. THEORETICAL UNITY

HEGEL joins the aesthetic together with his other philosophical subjects in a system with no fixed categories.[1] Consequently, the correlation he makes between art and knowledge is at once less tentative and less complete than made by Kant and Schopenhauer. Hegel does not distinguish between different kinds of cognitions, as does Kant in his distinction between understanding, reason, and judgment; nor does he divide the world into phenomena and essence, each with its separate way of being known, as does Schopenhauer. For Hegel, knowledge is all one, and its compartmentalizations are only historical way stations in its striving toward unity. The usual distinctions between realms of inquiry, between science, ethics, art, are also provisional and thus subject to later revision. All symbolic processes, for Hegel, are ways of knowing because he regards all process as symbolic. The distinction, in oether words, between nature and mind is itself provisional. The common content underlying the particular contents of different symbols is the incremental nature of change. Change is incremental because it has a direction—"process as progress"—and this notion of all reality as process directed toward a rational end, a "telos," is Hegel's famous principle: the "evolution of spirit."[2] In what follows, I look at these central themes in some detail, after which, in good Hegelian fashion, I locate the aesthetic through its contributions to the unity that his philosophy demands.

2. THE EVOLUTION OF SPIRIT

Hegel, although a contemporary of Schopenhauer, appears to have paid him little attention. But he was much influenced by Kant—although he took pains to establish himself as Kant's successor, not his disciple. In fact, the Hegelian philosophy presents a direct challenge to the Kantian critical system, and is thereby crucial to opening the nineteenth-century to the speculative methodology of idealism. This challenge is primarily directed at the epistemic tradition that Kant systematizes through his noumenal-phenomenal distinction. For Hegel, veridical representations of the world are not limited by sense data as they are for Kant, nor does he divide reality into separate realms with separate ways of knowing as does Schopenhauer. Hegel sees thought and the world as unified, which unity both constitutes reality and becomes increasingly adequate to reality in its (self-) perfection through time. This seeming contradiction, between constituting and knowing, is sustainable if we do not consider reality as that to which thought strives to become adequate, but rather as the inadequacy of incompleteness in both thought *and* its referent. This process of mutual completing in time is the sense of Hegel's thesis that the real is the rational. Knowledge at any given historical moment is limited and, thus, partial and imperfect. But the pressure such imperfection exerts gives rise to a more inclusive construal of knowing that in turn is exposed for its own inadequacies—and the process continues. For Hegel, limited knowledge, at whatever stage, is not "wrong" or "false" or "illusory"; rather, it represents a phase of development that is necessary to the continuation of the process, and thus, its content is not discarded but "taken up"—both retained and transformed—by the requirements of the succeeding stage.[3]

The historical course is directed toward overcoming partialities in the content of knowledge and increasing the unity between its forms. The Hegelian principle that governs this progressive unification is the "evolution of spirit," which can be identified in this context as the thread of intelligible purpose that unifies temporal sequence: the evidence in nature of a final cause and, by extension, of a divinity. The epistemic instrument through which we become aware of this purpose, the telic nature of time and history, Hegel identifies as "reason," but his is a very different instrument from the faculty within which Kant locates a priori judgments. For Kant, a priori judgments are "about" the world in the respect that they establish the *form* of empirical judgments, but their own justification, their "possibility," is by reference to the world beyond sensory experience—the noumenon—a world that Kant states we cannot know. For Hegel, the Kantian attribution of existence to a noumenal reality we cannot know is a philosophical absurdity.[4] To the contrary, Hegel argues that there is no noumenon, that the world we know is the only world there is, and that knowledge of ultimate reality is not only possible, it is inevitable. Such inevitability is provided by the thesis that, as knowledge is of the rational *as* the real, the process of achieving knowlege is tantamount to the reunion of thought and the world. The prefix "re" suggests the theological thesis that this union can also be considered the eschatological reunion of God and humanity and, as such, it is the "end" to which all process is directed.

In theorizing toward this ultimate unity, Hegel is unwilling to countenance any hard distinctions along the way: The traditional distinction between "matter and spirit" is recast into a transformation wherein matter gradually overcomes its "inertness" and is incorporated into spirit. The conflict between "individual and collective" is resolved by restricting the notion of true individuality to its function in the development of the group. Our standard two-valued logic is challenged by the addition of the mediating value "both . . . and . . . " to the exclusionary "or" that separates "true" from "false." And, famously, the struggles between empires, however bloody, always resolve for the better because in the, often unforeseeable, long run, struggle always correlates with greater unity. Because of the "inevitability" upon which his optimism depends, Hegel's theory is sometimes interpreted as an apologetic for Christian theology.[5] But this interpretation is open to question: Hegel's optimism is not "otherworldly" in the sense that it dualistically pits the world against a heavenly corrective. Then too, Hegel's invariable tendency to conflate opposites could even presume the eventual unity of heaven and earth, either as a secular, historical unity in the Marxist mode or as a unity consequent on conflations that Christianity would not accept: spirit and matter, thought and being—even good and evil. For Hegel, evil is passive; it is inertia—a lack of movement or a partiality in structure—and, as such, does not have the stature of a fundamental (diabolical) opposition to good. All obstacles that might be attributed to the workings of evil are susceptible to resolution through reason. There is no inscrutability, no doubt, as regards the outcome: Hegel's system does not require "faith" to guarantee its completion; for him, reason has no epistemic limits. Finally, it is not clear that Hegel conceives of God as distinct from this process of unification: His God might just *be* the end—the success—of spirit's evolution.[6]

Both Kant and Hegel identify "freedom" as a major philosophical value: Freedom is reason's instrument for "free will" in the Enlightenment, and it is also the instrument behind "progress" in historicism. Kant places the locus of freedom in rational morality; Hegel identifies it as reason in history.[7] Of course, Kant does not deny the possibility of historical progress; he has hopes that things will get better, that ideal values will actually become manifest in the world. But this hope is itself an ideal, a version of reflective judgment, and we cannot actually know, given Kant's epistemic restrictions, whether the wanted betterments are a matter of generations or millenia, or whether they will come at all.[8] For Kant, the time of rationality is not the time of history, and the value of moral freedom turns on its independence from the contingencies of historical events.

Hegel, to the contrary, locates freedom in the dialectic of historical change. Because such change is consonant with progress, historical process is freedom's source, and the full realization of freedom marks history's "end." Hegelian history has a variable rhythm; it moves faster as we approach the present. Its most proximate stage, the history of the Christian west, not only contains more radical transformations than do the earlier stages, but the most extreme transformations seem to have crowded into Hegel's own lifetime. He describes this acceleration as the extension of the principle of progress into its concept, the development of "self-consciousness." Freedom in later culture is not only more manifest but more overt, awareness as well as fact.

Acceleration within history suggests the proximate attainability of ideals, and this, in turn, breeds impatience. Thus, impatience becomes the mark of late history, and it is generated by the belief—typical of modernism—that the conditions of freedom can, and should, be reached within one's lifetime. Hegel contends that it is in the nature of freedom that its conditions are not to be had without a struggle. This is true for all realms: science, art, governance. Accordingly, the dialectical pattern of change, the forces in conflict, needs to be specified for each realm. Here, my concern is with the aesthetic.

3. ART AND NATURE

In the realm of the aesthetic, the first conflict is between nature and art, the second is between the various art forms, and the third is between the realm of art and the other ways of symbolizing the world. I follow Hegel's own sequence by treating these conflicts in turn.

Where Kant values nature above art, Hegel reverses this and dismisses natural beauty as a primitive manifestation of an order that is more highly, because consciously, developed in art. The constancy of natural beauty, which permits Kant to use it as a symbol of nature's essential order, is precisely the characteristic that, for Hegel, makes it inferior to the beauties of art. In the Hegelian framework, nature is valuable primarily because its constancy gives us a "point of origin" against which we can plot the successes and failures of our efforts at its transcendence. However attractive it may be, nature remains the repository of matter prior to its articulation by human consciousness; its beauty is only the precursor—the harbinger—of art. Thus, the Kantian move to share nature's timelessness through a "disinterested" appreciation is, in the Hegelian framework, a theoretical error. Kant places a higher aesthetic value on the resistance of natural beauty to concepts than he does on the impulse of artistic beauty to transcend the (conceptual) limitations of its own materiality. Hegel reverses this. Indeed, his *Aesthetics* begins with this statement: "The beauty of art is *higher* than nature. The beauty of art is beauty *born of the spirit and born again*, and the higher the spirit and its productions stand above nature and its phenomena, the higher too is the beauty of art above that of nature."[9] However, despite this early indication that the proper subject of aesthetics is art, Hegel does not deny beauty to nature. He examines this attribution with some care, and the result is a hierarchy of natural beauty that has some similarities to Schopenhauer's schema of the instantiations of the will.

In Schopenhauer's schema, nature is "graded" on an ascending scale of complexity from inanimate forms, through biological life, to human consciousness. Hegel, in his analysis of natural beauty, also distinguishes three levels: from discrete physical bodies, to aggregates of higher complexity, to biological forms of life; but Hegel excludes human beauty from nature. The comparison between the two theories is somewhat complex, but a distinction can be drawn between Schopenhauer's philosophical dualism, within which humans at once inhabit the world of nature and the world of essence, and Hegel's holism, where spiritual—thus, artistic—beauty only occurs through the manifestations of self-consciousness. And of these manifestations, the (self-) representation of self-consciousness is the symbolizing task given to art. One supposes here that, for Schopenhauer, the essences that constitute the content of art are all of a piece, sharing as they do their emancipations from the will, and thus human beauty is not different *in kind* (although it is in value) from the beauty of sunsets or stones.[10] Hegel must be interpreted differently: While, in one sense, the "evolution of spirit" begins with the creation of the world and is thus continuous and all encompassing, yet that point where spirit becomes not only "in" but "for" itself—when it is manifest as the human "soul"—marks a difference in kind from all that has gone before.[11] Human beauty is the sensuous presentation of this difference; it is the beauty of self-awareness and, thus, cannot be included with the beauties of nature.

4. ART AND THE IDEAL

In the Hegelian aesthetic, art is both absolute and relative. It is absolute because its subject is "the absolute"—of which the artistic version is "the ideal"; and it is relative because art presents this ideal through the historical evolution of style. There is a dense interweaving of terms and referents here: "absolute," "idea," "ideal," "spirit," "mind," "divine," et cetera. Sometimes they perform as synonyms, but often Hegel uses them to mark different levels of the interchange between thought and world.[12] For my limited purposes, the common referent of these terms is understood to be Hegel's metaphysical principle of the unity through which all diversities are reconciled. This principle, in its most comprehensive form, Hegel calls "spirit." Its logical, abstract form, as grasped purely in thought, is called the "idea." The sensuous manifestation of this principle in art Hegel calls the "ideal." Art symbolizes the effort of reconciliation and formally exemplifies it as historical fact. The subject of art is not its apparent content, the multiplicity of things depicted or described, but the bringing together of these things through the agency of artistic form. The ideality of art is this image of successful reconciliation, an encouragement, as it were, to our efforts at bringing unity to the world we live in—an image of achievable perfection. But art, great art, not only unifies what it represents, but presents itself as a unity—through its own formal perfection. Thus, art is both a thing in the world and a conceptual ideal. As an ideal, it can be considered a didactic tool of the "divine"—an epistemic model, so to speak, of the "absolute." As a thing, art is subject to historical change.

Relativizing the absolute in art is not to be taken as a denial of the former or a weakening of the latter, only as a recognition of Hegel's thesis that the evolution of spirit is an unfolding in time. This thesis indicates that while art is absolute in its individual works, it is relative through its history, the stylistic interdependency of its works. The issue, here, is not the perfection of art; it is, given that perfection, how art can be said to "progress." The Hegelian notion of artistic progress is a complex one, for it combines *what can best be done,* the notion of quality, with *what it is possible to do,* the notion of historical limitation. This is both an aesthetic and a philosophical limitation. While Hegel expands art by giving it an epistemic function, he also delimits it by correlating its epistemic efficacy with its historical position. The tension between aesthetic and epistemic can be presented in this way: To the extent that progress in art parallels the development of cultures, the best art is that which most adequately symbolizes its own time; but since cultural development is also progressive, art that is from "advanced" cultures supersedes art of earlier cultures through differences in both characteristic form and referential scope. Do these differences constitute a difference in aesthetic value? The answer is a Hegelian "yes and no."

Hegel characterizes the differences between cultures as specific resolutions of the tension between matter and spirit. These historical ratios also serve to categorize artworks into kinds and styles, and to link them to the historical accomplishments of their individual cultures. Thus, each culture has its own optimal artistic symbol. But spirit is the ascendant principle throughout the history of culture, and art symbolizes its progressive victories. Notwithstanding the historical changes in its symbolic mission, art remains throughout a sensuous symbol—which is both the identity and limitation Hegel gives it. And spirit is, well, spirit—whose chronicling, at some late point of "dematerialization," will exhaust the epistemic capacities of art. Cultural and artistic development, therefore, are not identical: As a symbol, art can aspire to a value that culture cannot; namely, art can evidence an equilibrium, a perfect harmony, in its allotted ratio of matter and spirit. This is independent of historical change and marks the possibility of absolute value in art. Culture, on the other hand, is always in disequilibrium, for its material-spiritual mix is transient, an ongoing conflict between achievement become moribund and aspiration that seeks actuality. To the degree that art is a symbol of that conflict, it is transitional and, thus, normatively relative.

5. CLASSIFICATION OF THE ARTS

Hegel's classification of the arts is both a chronology and a conceptual schema, although it is not always clear which one is at issue at any given point. His basis is the division of historical art into three great periods—or "forms"—of art, which he calls "Symbolic," "Classic," and "Romantic." The first corresponds to the art of the ancient Far and Middle East: India, Egypt, and the cultures of the Old Testament; the second primarily contains the geographically limited art of classical Greece; the third comprises the art of the Christian West from its origins to Hegel's own time.

The thread on which Hegel's "forms of art" are strung is the artistic aspect of the battle between matter and spirit. The history of this aspect—art history—chronicles the changing disequilibrium between these principles through the changing equilibriums of artworks. As art's subject is the ideal, its task is to transform matter from encumbrance to image. In the earliest form, the Symbolic, the disequilibrium favors the inertness of material, or "medium," against an as yet inchoate spiritual content. The urge to express what cannot yet be known creates an art that Hegel variously describes as "distorted," "grotesque," "bizzare," "gigantic"—descriptions through which he also characterizes the gods of the ancient Indian and archaic Greek mythologies.[13] But these characterizations are more classificatory than judgmental. They serve to contrast historical versions of the ideal, although Hegel does not always distinguish between his own tastes and those appropriate to the overview he seeks. But, in the main, Hegel's evaluative framework echoes the complexity of his historical scheme: The art form whose value may be greater from one standpoint, the evolution of spirit, may be differently assessed from another standpoint, the "absoluteness" of art. This tension between values is evident in Hegel's reference to the "hidden" content of Symbolic art, what could be called the content of the intent rather than of the image.[14] He thus tempers his nineteenth-century distaste for archaic and primitive art with his philosophical interest in the potency of its spiritual quest.

The second of Hegel's three forms of art, the Classical, comprises the arts of ancient Greece from that point in the early classical period where the archaic style had lost its influence to that early point in Hellenistic art where the stable equilibrium of high classicism had been skewed but not yet dissolved.[15] Hegel professes for this form a particular admiration that is missing in his treatment of the other two. One reason for this admiration may simply be nostalgia for a "golden age," as can be found in the general infatuation, in Hegel's Germany, with everything Greek. But the more important reason is theoretical; it is the place of the Classical form in Hegel's system. Hegel considered it the "perfect art," one in which matter and spirit are in complete equilibrium—where the sensuous manifestation of the "idea" is neither excessive in its concreteness nor wanting in its attenuation. This perfection is not a matter of art's showing what we can know, for on that score, the later Romantic art is more valuable. Rather, it is classical art's complete adequacy, as a sensuous symbol, in showing what was then known. The polytheistic Greek gods of the third century B.C. were equally—if precariously—human and divine. Through this equilibrium, they gave art a content—the idealized human figure—that it fully satisfied as both form and implication.

If the disequilibrium in Symbolic art favors the physical principle, that of the Romantic form is tilted toward the spiritual.[16] The monotheistic Christian God begins in history by taking on human form. But this godly "reification" is not the balanced one of classicism, for here it serves to illuminate the spiritual side of human nature and, thus, begins the process of disengagement between the artistic image and its physical vehicle. The early historical stages of this process are marked by a new antagonism beteen matter and spirit: the Christian ascetic's "abnegation of flesh" and "disdain for worldly goods." But for Hegel, newly aggressive dualities are not to be overcome by simply choosing between them: Matter is not to be summarily rejected; it is, like all partialities, to be "taken up"—given new form—within a historically higher unity.

It is worth noting, parenthetically, that the residue of this transformative process, what is left behind, also has a kind of (recidivistic) unity; it successfully combines material excess with theoretical irrelevance. This is the negative value in Hegel's system, for it marks the inertial factor that inhibits progress. In modernism, this factor becomes an ideologically overt issue through the many accusations that are leveled against the academic art and social stratifications of the time. I take this up in Chapter Seven.

6. THE PARTICULAR ARTS

The particular arts weave through Hegel's forms of art by contrasting their individual historical developments with their roles as symbols for the dominant values of each form. Hegel identifies five particular arts: architecture, sculpture, painting, music, poetry; and he assigns to each a primary exemplifying role for a form of art.

Architecture is the major Symbolic art, and its products are best exampled by the temples of India and the pyramids of Egypt. Although Hegel recognizes the many painted and sculpted evocations of the ancient deities of those times, he considers them ancillary to the main thrust of the Symbolic form: to provide "dwellings" for a god who has not yet arrived, whose nature is only knowable in the abstract. It should be noted that Hegel's use here of the term "abstract" is pejorative, for it signifies inadequacy and inchoateness. This usage is very different from the positive value given to "abstract" in modernism, where it signifies the purification or transcendence of representational imagery. Hegel's antonym to "abstract" is "concrete," which he sees as a historical achievement of specificity, mutual adequacy, between form and content. Further care must be taken, however, to distinguish Hegel's "concreteness" from his "materiality," the latter merely being a symptom of the inadequacies that cause "abstractness."

In the Symbolic form, the temple for an absent god identifies God's "otherness"—the antipodal relationship between an inscrutable God and a humanity that worships as a duty without hope for communion. It is here that Hegel locates the notion of the "sublime": The attempt at imaging a god that is not known can only result in conceptual, if not aesthetic, grotesqueries. Actually, according to Hegel, such a god can best be philosophically expressed through the *absence* of images. One remembers here that, in the Kantian experience of the sublime, the mind draws away from sensibility and, instead, substitutes an idea: a delimiting idea of the infinite. Hegel identifies such a process, the withdrawal of mind back into itself, with ancient Hebrew poetry and identifies these works as the "strict" expression of the Symbolic form. These works "cancel the positive immanence of the Absolute in its created phenomena and put the *one* substance explicitly apart as Lord of the world in contrast to whom there stands the entirety of his creatures, and these, in comparison with God, are posited as the inherently powerless and perishable. . . . We no longer find here any Indian distortion into the shapelessness of the boundless."[17] This ability to *conceive* of divinity as absolute otherness is—even more than with Kant—the solace that sublimity provides: the self-respect of mind that is generated by its own capacities.

The art of the next form, the Classical, softens this absolute contrast by correlating a different concept of divinity with a uniquely compatible image. The concept is of an anthropomorphic and polytheistic divinity—the Greek gods—and the form is the human, predominantly nude figure presented in carved sculpture. These rationally proportional "ideal" forms inhabit the same space, and often have the same scale, as do actual persons; through this they exemplify the special equivalence between matter and spirit that Hegel sees as the primary content of Classical art.

This notion of equivalence is also to be found in the Kantian aesthetic judgment, specifically, in Kant's characterization of beautiful nature as "purposive without purpose." Here, the harmony, the equilibrium, between form and sensation neutralizes the conflict between intelligibility and feeling, and frees us from the need for either action or withdrawal. For Kant, beauty is a momentary and transient perfection, a hiatus, in our otherwise purpose-ridden lives, much as, for Hegel, Classical sculpture is also a hiatus, for it symbolizes a historical moment of truce in the cultural strife between spirit and its material inhibitions.

It is in the nature of Hegel's philosophizing that he assign different values to his historical protagonists when he views them from different vantage points. While the art of classical Greece may be the perfect art qua art, it is not the highest, most "advanced," art because such perfection is transient and must yield to the destabilizing dynamics of progress. The conditions of artistic perfection are also the conditions of cultural inertia: The Greek city-states are eventually overcome and their art is scattered in replica and mannered adaptation throughout the Roman Empire.

The equipoise between stability and gesture in Classical sculpture, that internal harmony between presence and meaning that also marks a harmony between individuals and their social stations—a primary virtue in Plato's *Republic*—does not fully reemerge until the time of the Christian Renaissance. There it is represented through the art of painting, the first of the Romantic arts. This shift from the physical three-dimensionality of stone to the three-dimensionality of planar illusion is, for Hegel, a further victory of spirit over matter. This victory directs aesthetic content into the subjective values of individual witness befitting the new nature of divinity: a god that is "triune" and immanent. Hegel describes the transition from the Classical to the Romantic form in this way: "The story of the Passion . . . is separated *toto caelo* from the classical because here the subject matter itself implies that the external bodily appearance, immediate existence as an individual, is revealed in the grief of his negativity as the negative, and that therefore it is by sacrificing subjective individuality and the sensuous sphere that the Spirit attains its truth and its Heaven."[18]

The first Romantic art, painting, is able to supersede the physical concreteness of sculpture because within pictorial space, the illusionistic representation of three-dimensionality, the separate demands of (old) objective and (new) subjective contents can be bridged. The innocent sculptural robustness of the gods *as* human, however ideal, gives way to the mystery of God *become* human. The direction of this "becoming" is not a concession to matter, however; it moves the other way. For Hegel, the advent of Christianity is a harbinger of a new possibility, namely, the spiritual reconciliation of human and divine. This possibility is built on the subjective contents of the Passion: sacrifice, sorrow, forgiveness, love. And painting, through its representational capacity for mood, allusion, and even the suggestion of passing time, takes on that content and thus begins Hegel's third form of the arts.

But the demands of the new subjectivity are inexorable, and painting fulfills them at only one point in its history—in the religious art of da Vinci, Titian, and, especially, Raphael. The later turn of painting to secular subjects is not so much a sign of aesthetic disvalue as an indication, for Hegel, of the symbolic limits of that art. Content evolves beyond the capacity of pictorial representation. Hegel puts it this way: "But if the inner life, as is already the case in the principle of painting, is in fact to be manifested as a *subjective* inwardness, the genuinely correspondent material cannot be of such a kind that it persists on its own account. . . . the obliteration not of *one* dimension only (as in painting) but of the whole of space, purely and simply, this complete withdrawal, of both the inner life and its expression, into subjectivity, brings into being the *second* Romantic art—music."[19] So, music is prized because, as a nonrepresentational art, it can present the subjective life of "feelings." In this view, Hegel and Schopenhauer are remarkably alike. They both correlate the flow of music with the experience of the self in time, and the dynamics and sonorities of music with the content of this experience. In Hegel's terms, "all nuances of cheerfulness and serenity, the sallies, moods and jubilations of the soul, the degrees of anxiety, misery, mourning, lament, sorrow, grief, longing, etc., and lastly of awe, worship, love, etc., become the peculiar sphere of musical expression."[20] This passage could easily support Schopenhauer's construal of music as a representation of "the will itself."

However, Hegel never quite separated the value of musical content from the contributions of lyrics—the verbal aspect of music in songs, oratorios, operas, et cetera. Indeed, he looked with some suspicion on what he called "independent" music, arguing that without the conceptual safeguards that textual materials supply, music is prone to become increasingly formalistic and, therefore, subject to "eccentricities" and "deceptive agitations."[21] In this, he echoes Kant. The normative alliance between music and discourse marks a historical as well as a theoretical juncture. For Hegel, the grand tradition of music peaks in the eighteenth-century, particularly with Mozart; and this also indicates music's limitations as a Romantic art—that musical subjectivity finally becomes a hindrance to the new content that the poetic text alone can express: the world of "concrete actuality."[22]

In Hegel's system, poetry, as the successor to music in the Romantic form, is, by virtue of that position, the most advanced of the arts, the particular art expressing the highest truths that art, as a symbolic form, is capable of. Poetry is an art of discourse, and thus, its sensuality is not in its medium but in its imagery; it is the most "dematerialized" of the arts. Hegel scrutinizes poetry more extensively than he does the other arts, and he uses the term quite broadly, dividing it (yet again) into three parts—epic, lyric, and dramatic—each part stretching through all of history while reaching such peaks as the Greek epics, the odes of Horace, and the dramas of Shakespeare and Goethe.

Poetry differs from all other arts because it is in the medium of rational discourse—also the medium of philosophy. It remains art because, although discursive, it does not assert; its truths are interpreted for reason by imagination and feeling. As the last and highest art of the Romantic form, poetry synthesizes—again in the sense of "taking up"—the particular capacities of all the other arts. Hegel puts it this way: "Poetry, the art of speech, is the third term, the totality, which unites in itself, within the province of the spiritual inner life and on a higher level, the two extremes,i.e., the visual arts and music. For, on the one hand, poetry, like music, contains that principle of the self-apprehension of the inner life as inner, which architecture, sculpture, and painting lack; while, on the other hand, in the very field of inner ideas, perceptions, and feelings, it broadens out into an objective world which does not altogether lose the determinate character of sculpture and painting. Finally, poetry is more capable than any other art of completely unfolding the totality of an event, a successive series and the changes of the heart's movements, passions, ideas, and the complete course of action."[23] One recalls here that in Hegel's originary form, the Symbolic, the purest exemplar is the poetic sublime, because the god then in question was too distant, too abstract to be imaged. Now, in the Romantic form, the schema ends—again with poetry—but this time because the god in question is too immediate, too interior to be imaged.

7. DIFFICULTIES

Hegel's view of art history, and history in general, has been subject to much criticism. The more telling criticisms reject the "moral" of Hegel's narrative, the notion that history has a direction, purpose, and goal, and the notion that this moral applies equally to the future as to the past.[24] The scope of such criticism goes beyond my subject, but one difficulty should be indicated here: All of Hegel's basic themes are narratives of development—whether of rationality, culture, art, or religion. All these narratives interweave conceptual values with historical events, and in order to ensure a fit, Hegel often adjusts fact to concept. Whatever one's sympathies with Hegel's underlying teleology, this tension beween chronological and conceptual sequence creates certain problems: How, for example, does one evaluate individual works of art in those periods when their types are not dominant? If Hegel's schema is construed as purely historical, it would have to follow, for example, that architecture, as an art, declined in value after the pyramids, and that poetry did not reach its highest development until, say, Goethe. On the other hand, if Hegel's preferences are read structurally rather than chronologically, if, for example, poetry's affinity with philosophical discourse is, as such, more valuable than architecture's dependency on material gravity, then poetry has *always* been the highest—although, only recently, the most exemplary—art. Looking further at Hegel's schema, such difficulties compound, and ever more elaborate maneuvers are needed to maintain credibility. Hegel himself would probably not have considered this a problem, perceiving the need to shift judgmental bases back and forth, as different issues come up, as yet another demonstration of the emerging unity between thought and the world. And *this* truth, Hegel might say, can withstand any factual challenge.

Hegel had a scope of historical knowledge that neither Kant nor Schopenhauer, nor, indeed, few others in his time, could match, and yet he denied that the amassing of historical facts amounts to a historical narrative. To the contrary, he believed that the telic structure of historical change identifies just those facts that are, indeed, historical.[25] On this point, one could say that Hegel was prescient in anticipating later notions that there are no "historical facts" independent of contexts of narration.[26] Modernist versions of Hegel's theory of artistic progress, while not so unremittingly teleological as his, all share the belief that historical, particularly art-historical, narratives select the facts that, in turn, demonstrate their truth.

8. ARTISTIC CREATIVITY

I conclude this discussion of Hegel's aesthetics with some remarks on his construal of artistic creativity. This is not an issue he discusses at any length, and its importance for his aesthetic theory lies in the intersection of individual creativity and the imperatives of history. This direction of theory provides the distinction between Hegel's artist and those of Kant and Schopenhauer. In his metaphysics, Hegel rejects the thesis of a noumenal reality beyond appearances; accordingly, he has no need for a Kantian "nature's voice" to fashion images affirming that reality. The epistemic value that Schopenhauer places on individual artistic expression is also of little use to Hegel except in determining which expression truly images, not the irrational will, but the rationality of historical progress. Hegel's discussion of artistic creativity centers on his insistence that such creativity not be deflected from its task of creating historically significant art. In this respect, he is closer to the Kantian view of the artist as a vehicle for producing symbols that have a philosophically important content. Schopenhauer's concern with the psychology of this effort, as itself containing value, does not appear in Hegel.

For his account, Hegel divides the subject in familiar triadic fashion. His categories, simplified, are "genius," "objectivity," and "style"; and, for each, he identifies failings that would limit the depth and direction of the undertaking. Thus, genius is other than, although it includes, mere "talent"; the objectivity of an artist's view is more than, although it must satisfy, the technical need for accuracy in depiction or description; and style, although it develops through originality, goes beyond the personal eccentricities of "manner." None of this is particularly debatable—because it is so general—and Hegel only specifies his remarks by pointing at great artworks that, because of their value, are evidently the result of a properly calibrated creativity. Here, as with Kant, one finds the genius through the work.[27]

Hegel takes pains to differentiate the artistic process from the process of philosophizing, but the former is, in a sense, captive to the latter, for neither creativity nor its products can deny, or be indifferent to, philosophy's imperative: the inevitability of spirit's progress. A notorious Hegelian thesis is that the course of history creates heroes and victims. It is notorious because, unlike "open-ended" construals of historical change in which what is valued accommodates what is wanted or feared, Hegel sees history as the kind of morality play in which wants and fears are subject to the inexorable demands of historical change. Through this subjection—better, subjugation—ultimate value rests in conformance with the pattern of change: An irrelevant life, however well meaning, is of no consequence, while an act that furthers the purposes of history, however self-serving, is exemplary. Hegel's "world-historical individual" does not confuse the values of personal history with the history of accomplishment and thus gains the universality that Kant's "genius" enjoys through the role of "nature's voice." This form of universality gives Hegel's artist the role of efficient cause in a normative account of historical change.

Given this role, the Kantian aesthetic value of fidelity to nature, later coupled with Schopenhauer's value of self-awareness, now takes on a new component: It is the belief that an artwork, however faithful to its subject or deeply felt by its creator, has little value if it does not anticipate the future. This belief is one of Hegel's bequests—his legacy—to the aesthetics of modernism.

II

THEMES AND TRANSFORMATIONS

FOUR

Kant and Taste

1. FOREWORD

MY CONCERN in this second part is more with the internal structure of the aesthetic theories under discussion than with their roles in the overall philosophical systems. In Part I, I locate these theories in the systematic concerns of Kant, Schopenhauer, and Hegel. Here, I trace their move away from these concerns into the more particular ones of aesthetics taken as a distinct area of study. I characterize each theory through a theme that is both a consolidation and a simplification of its earlier theoretical self—an appropriation of part of its earlier subject for itself, and a willingness to forgo the rest. Thus, these themes now speak more directly to the issues of art and criticism, and largely avoid the issue of ontic and epistemic obligation. In the course of this transformation, the philosophical antecedents of these themes become generational memories that are occasionally invoked—through piety, or sometime anxiety—but that more often are put aside for the usual generational reasons: tediousness and irrelevance. I identify these themes as "taste," "expression," and "progress," and their sources as, respectively, the aesthetics of Kant, Schopenhauer, and Hegel.

This is a transitional part of my study in which I look at these newly autonomized themes and note some characteristics and peculiarities of their contents. In the following part, I discuss their further transformations into the ideologies of modernism and postmodernism. Here, I focus on the roots of these transformations and on contrasts between them that anticipate the later polemics of ideology and style. I begin with an examination of some peculiarities of the term "taste" and then trace it through the Kantian aesthetic.

2. TASTE AS SENSE AND SENSIBILITY

Despite its ubiquity, and its prominence in Kantian theory, "taste" is a rather peculiar term for aesthetic contexts, since it refers to a sense that is ordinarily not associated with either art or beauty. Of course, taken in its exalted sense, taste—like "vision"—refers not merely to a sense but to a sensibility, and it thus acquires normative content: Kant's vision of a just society, his "kingdom of ends," may require that its inhabitants have good taste. Taken in its ordinary sense, however, this content is lacking: When something "tastes good," the sentiment does not transfer to its aesthetic counterpart, at least not in the way looking does in the appreciation of art and beauty. With due apologies to haute cuisine, there is no aesthetic continuity between the objects of taste taken through sense and those taken through sensibility. The objects of sense that do so transfer, those that constitute the realms of the visual and musical arts, are objects of sight and hearing. When aesthetic appreciation is limited to nature, a further reduction is implied: For the capacity to perceive natural beauty, sight seems most fundamental—the configurations of clouds and branches giving us more in this regard than the sound of the wind. In the appreciation of the natural sublime, however, sight and sound seem more nearly equal, for what would tempests and torrents be without their roar?

Of course, these difficulties in correlating the sense of taste with aesthetic objects also extends to smell and touch. Why the history of aesthetics chose taste as its arbiter instead of these others is an interesting but digressive question, so I leave it with the sole observation that taste seems more volitional than the others.

When we say, "A vision of beauty," we identify a sensible universal—beauty instantiated. Under this usage, "A taste of beauty" is either incoherent or a gag. Evidently, then, the "taste" in aesthetic taste separates from its ordinary literal usage; it is a metaphor that derives its power from a more specialized literal context. As such, it plays a powerful role in the Kantian aesthetic and a partisan role in that aesthetic's later development. I approach this version of "taste," its use as a specifically aesthetic metaphor, through some further thoughts on its literal origins.

There is something hesitant about (merely) tasting: It is an act that moves forward and then pulls away; it does not really confront its object. Perhaps taste has no object, only a subject—or, perhaps, a subject that willingly separates from its object.[1] To "taste something" does not require that we eat or drink it; the vocations of chefs and sommeliers depend on this distinction. Tasting is characterized by small movements, and it is most easily (accurately) done when we are neither hungry nor thirsty, when we do not desire what we taste. Actually, culinary morsels of great appeal, those that stir up feral memories, require forbearance at all times—if the task of tasting is indeed to estimate rather than consume. It should follow, then, that those who exercise "good taste" are always slightly hungry; they do not consume what they consider, for their concern has shifted from the satisfaction of appetite to the contemplation of its subject. Now, if we were to limit satisfaction to satiation, we might agree that this is inimical to the exercise of taste; gluttony, for example, is circumscribed only by the legalities of possession. However, this is not to say that taste countermands its own satisfaction, only that the satisfaction is of a different kind, one that works against—indeed, requires the suppression of—the inclination to consume or possess. Such satisfaction is of taste, not as sense, but as (aesthetic) sensibility.

Given this distinction, I move to some further considerations of taste in Kant's aesthetics. My concern here is with differences in the exercise of taste in nature and in art, and with some implications of this for later theory.

3. TASTE IN NATURE AND ART

Kant identifies taste as the "faculty of judging of the beautiful," and he devotes the bulk of his analysis of beauty to a discussion of the criteria for the exercise of that faculty.[2] As I indicate in Chapter One, these criteria are specified in the "four moments" of the "Analytic of the Beautiful" and divide into two pairs: the logical requirements of "universality" and "necessity," and the psychological requirements of "disinterestedness" and "purposiveness." The first pair establishes the scope and modality of the judgment, and it concerns the compatibility of reflection, given its synthesizing task, with the logical forms of both empirical knowledge and morality. This speaks to the systematic role of Kant's aesthetic. The second pair regulates the attitude of the spectator and the subject of appreciation. Here, the concern is with the actual exercise of taste, and the appropriateness of various things in the world to that exercise.

The taste in question is, of course, "good taste," that is, the taste of "sensibility," there being no other kind having philosophical importance for Kant.[3] And the capacity for aesthetic appreciation seems to be synonymous with it. Viewing taste through the requirement of disinterestedness supports the remarks above that we should neither wish to possess what we appreciate nor explain it away. Instead, we are merely to savor it without diminishing it and consider it without subsuming it under rules, for appreciation is successful only when we are free of the practical implications of our experience.

For Kant, aesthetic judgment is concerned with neither the uses nor, even, the existence of appreciation's physical object, only with its representation. "Purposiveness," the quality consequent on a disinterested appreciation, is actually to be found in the image and only hopefully in the object—that hope being more a theoretical than a practical desideratum. Given this, Kant does separate appreciation's objects into two basic subjects, nature and art, and here the question arises as to how taste functions in these two appreciations—whether, despite the seeming synonymy between taste and appreciation, there are differences in application to their subjects and where these differences might lie.

I approach this question by first looking at taste in the appreciation of nature. A perfect appreciation in Kant can be compared to his concept of perfect goodness: both are ideals, necessary for the validity of the concept, but unattainable in actual situations. As no individual can completely separate duty from private interests, so none can wholly rid appreciation of the taint of desire. Kant remarks that it is easier to do one's duty when one has no feelings for the party concerned, for then moral obligation is most clearly distinguished from all other reasons for action.[4] Similarly, in appreciation, success is best attained when the subject is not of the kind to be possessed, for then we can admire it—"taste" it—without being deflected by acquisitiveness. On this score, consider Kant's penchant for landscape as the prime exemplar of natural beauty. Directed at this subject, the exercise of taste requires both means and leisure: a stroll in the countryside without concern for time wasted, needs unfulfilled, or opportunities missed. The mind can then be freed to contemplate nature's harmonies and imagine them of a kind with the harmonies of the self. Aesthetic appreciation in this optimal context is a sort of practice for how to behave when things become trying, when harmony between the self's parts is difficult to maintain.

When we turn to the relationship between taste and artistic beauty, however, we find that the "ideal spectator" of beautiful nature takes on another persona—that of the "connoisseur" or "patron." But in this context things may indeed be trying and harmony elusive. Kant believes that the best art is that which most seems like nature.[5] However, to appreciate art as one does nature, that is to say, disinterestedly, would require that one forswear the urge for possession. Yet, it seems evident that the acquisitive urge of patronage is central to the history of art and its appreciation. Of course, against this conflation of interest and art, one could argue that great public museums and concert halls are, in fact, much like landscapes where one goes to taste the beauties of art without heed to their commodification. One could then regard these institutions not as social extensions of the core practices of patronage, but as social alternatives—expiations, if you will—that function to counter these practices by returning art to its proper status as a subject of the exercise of taste. In this regard, it should be remembered that Kant lived before the era of the great public museums, at a time when access to masterworks, indeed, to most art, required a social status comparable to or, at least, compatible with those who owned such works. He did not see the public projections of art that marked the rise of bourgeois culture. Whether this later construal of the museum as "art's landscape" would give Kant reason to put aside his hesitations about art's aesthetic purity, whether, that is, he would consider the democratization of access to art an enhancing of the autonomy of taste, or whether he would see it as an unhappy victory for the pairing of taste and commodification, is a speculative question, but an interesting one.

4. TASTE, STYLE, AND HISTORY

There is another fractious issue in Kant's application of taste to the appreciations of nature and art that invokes a central issue in Hegelian aesthetics. I present it with that inflection: Artistic tastes are directed toward style, and style is a temporal phenomenon—successions of artifacts and commentaries that document cultural and historical change. Despite formalist protestations that speak to the insularity and self-sufficiency of artistic traditions (see Chapter Seven), the interpretations that normatively categorize artworks cannot but reflect other, nonaesthetic preferences in the societies of their origin. Taste in art, in its public, critical, form, decides between works whose claims to excellence are based upon competing criteria. As these aesthetic conflicts are metaphors for instabilities in the larger society, preferences in art can be seen as predictive of social change. There is then a correlation to be made between aesthetic value and the actual direction of change.

Kant, of course, does not accept any such relativity between judgments of taste, particularly when they apply to nature. In that realm, the presumption is one of timelessness—a repudiation of the intrusions of style so that the image of nature's unity can be perceived as eternal and unchanging. The natural vistas that do *not* work for such appreciation are the ones that show their style, those which cultivation has transformed from nature into art.[6] On this score as well, it would seem that for the Kantian aesthetic, taste in art is philosophically more peripheral than is taste for beauty in nature. Past art is compromised by the detritus of decided battles, and present art by the anxieties of ongoing ones. Here, the reference turns to the Kantian moments of universality and necessity: Art that depends on history for its value—and what art does not?—is inferior to nature in scope and modality. Art is only presumptively universal and necessary, for its objects are all rendered contingent by the passage of time. If, by a juxtaposition of past and future, one could position Kant's theory as a critique of Hegel's, one might well find the thesis that taste, when directed toward art, is compromised—made impure—by its dependency on historical contingency. For from that precarious position, an individual judgement of taste cannot effect, even for reflection, the desired synthesis of understanding and reason: Its particular instrument, some artwork, might, in the meantime, have been disvalued. In the Hegelian aesthetic, where understanding is subsumed under reason, and reason is only—progressively—actualized *within* history, there is no such limitation on art. To the contrary, nature, especially when rendered ahistorical through its separation from culture, incurs the onus of aesthetic inadequacy. Nature so separate, for Hegel, is not "pure," only "inert." It thus has only a negative consequence for the evolution of spirit.

There is, of course, continuity as well as disagreement between Hegel and Kant. One of the pathways to Hegel in Kant's aesthetics can be found by following his theory into the analysis of teleological judgment.[7] Teleology is also a form of reflective judgment and, as with beauty and sublimity, its role in the synthesis of understanding and reason is merely regulatory. Kant's aim, in his discussion of teleology, is to provide legitimacy for a nonmechanistic account of nature through a reflective finding that interprets natural change as purposeful evolution toward inherent ends. Thus, the extensional rationality provided nature by the judgment of beauty complements the durational rationality provided by teleology. However, Kant is also concerned with the possibility of moral evolution: the historical progress of societies toward a collective and universal good.[8] "Progress" is an a priori idea of reason, but so is the possibility of morality as such, and both concepts look to reflective judgment for their affirmation in the sensible realm. Kant uses the static architectonics of natural beauty to authenticate the theoretical existence of morality, but he is less clear about the purpose of art. So I propose an interpretation that moves his theory closer to the Hegelian aesthetic, namely, that the history of art viewed teleologically be used to ground the concept of moral progress.

The connection here between aesthetics and teleology can be put in this way: In the same sense that the moral law seeks its justification by appeal to a rationally structured nature, so does it seem futile to practice morality without the expectation that it will increasingly be a norm of future societies. Now, if the appreciation of beauty provides evidence of rationality in nature, might not the appreciation of art provide symbolic support for the expectation of social progress? Accepting this hypothesis would rescue artistic taste from its subordinate role, as a helpmate to natural beauty, by assigning it a different subject. Admittedly, Kant nowhere indicates that the aesthetic judgment could be split in this way, but an opening for just such an interpretation lies in his demand that creations of artistic genius be both exemplary *and* novel. Surely, this joining of value with novelty moves art into history. Consider the following: The appreciation of nature does not seem additive; insights achieved through the meditations of a Kantian walk in the woods are not deepened by walking through two woods. If we were to hold, then, that taste, whether directed at art or nature, is essentially the same, we might also suppose that what is *philosophically* important in art can be found in any one masterpiece. But it seems absurd to suppose, even in Kantian terms, that there is no philosophical reason for the multiplicity of art-historical works—no rational "task" at issue. One could conjecture that, for Kant, when nature is viewed from the standpoint of eternity, as an architectonic "ground" for rationality, its various appreciations merely provide *reaffirmations* for reflective judgment. However, when nature is viewed as process, as "evidence" of teleological progress, its ongoing appreciations *enlarge the content* of reflective judgment. Whether we interpret social teleology as a proper part of natural teleology or as a separate category, the above notion of enlargement seems equally to apply: Whatever it is that symbolizes moral progress, appreciation of its ongoing instances adds to our understanding of this process—but also, as Hegel would insist, it adds to the completion of the process itself.

I suggest here that when we take artworks to exemplify the telos of the social ideal, our interpretation approximates a Hegelian critique of Kant. The move is to overcome Kant's "regulatory" limitation on the thesis of moral progress by showing that it is symbolized by an actual, documentable, teleological process: progress in art. The point of this move, one that Kant might even have accepted, is to regard the thesis of social progress as supported by appeal to the normative evolution of its aesthetic symbols. Progress in art, then, becomes the "rational guarantee" for progress in culture.

5. GENIUS AND CONNOISSEURSHIP

For both Kant and Hegel, the exercise of taste entails a high level of historical optimism. The demand for universal agreement in value judgments about art must be based on the belief that "good taste" can identify, out of all that history contains, the works of true genius. In both theories, art's philosophical task is borne by the works of genius—not any artwork will do.[9] Thus, the exercise of taste must correlate with the winnowing process of history to accomplish that task. It would then seem that, even for Kant, historical sophistication is a necessary, if not sufficient, condition for aesthetic judgment as applied to art. This consideration moves us away from the conflict between the aesthetics of nature and art into the specific concern with taste in art. Here the question arises how one distinguishes between works of genius and lesser works, and what the philosophical consequences of this distinction are.

Consider again Kant's two main requirements for the works of "genius": They must be original, and they must be exemplary.[10] In the first requirement, Kant defines originality as a production "for which no rule can be given." Let us probe this a bit: The products of an activity that is not rule governed, to be original, must be "novel" in the sense that it is both new and unique. Mere newness will not do, for a thing can simply be the newest of its kind, the latest eggbeater to come off the line; and uniqueness alone is also not enough, since, even with the most familiar things, no two are exactly alike.

Nevertheless, originality in itself does not satisfy genius: Evidently, some things that are novel are merely bizarre or eccentric, and, for Kant, there would be little in such things to reflect upon. So a further distinction is needed, and we come to his second requirement, namely, that works of genius must be exemplary. Examples function to generate rules by which relevant similarities among things can be determined, and exemplary artworks do the same: They provide rules for our understanding of what artworks are like. However, this seems to conflict with the first criterion: As the requirement of novelty also applies to the creation of artworks of genius, it seems clear that such creations cannot be based on the rules generated by other exemplary works. This poses an epistemic dilemma for the connoisseur: How can one know whether a given novel work is exemplary? The very term "novel" has a Hegelian flavor, and the answer is also Hegelian: One cannot know—but one can predict. And the probability of being right, of distinguishing the masterpiece from merely eccentric works, depends on how well one understands the telic structure of historical change. Such understanding is not via a formal inference but is a kind of holistic intuition, one that Hegel, but not Kant, would consider truth generating. One structures the past—decides which of it is history—in order to predict its future. If history has a telic structure, then the probability of accord between it and our descriptions of its past is the same as the probability that our predictions of its future are true.

But this preoccupation with the future also seems suited to the theme of artistic creativity. Certainly, with a bit of personalizing, one could attribute to artists the Kantian "hope" that the novelty and uniqueness generated through their artworks will also prove exemplary. By locating this hope in both appreciation and creativity, however, does one make too little of the Kantian distinction between "taste" and "nature's voice"?

In examining the relation in Kant's aesthetics between connoisseur and artist—taste and creativity—one could argue that Kant's artist does not require taste, indeed, that the exercise of taste is inhibitory to creativity. In his characterization of artistic creativity, Kant indicates that if imaginative gifts of genius come into conflict with the disciplines of taste in the production of art, the latter must be discarded. On the other hand, in his analysis of the appreciation of art, taste is primary.[11]

The strictness of this distinction falters, however, when one considers that among the tasks of appreciation is the proposal of novel works *for* appreciation—the designation of some such works as candidates for the exercise of taste.[12] But if taste is guided by the properties of existing exemplary works, it will resist application to new original works. In this respect, one could say that taste is inhibitory to the connoisseur as well; it only apprehends exemplary works in hindsight—it cannot deal with novelty. So a new alliance suggests itself: not between appreciation and the exemplary work, but between appreciation and the creative act. The presumption here is that philosophical value is located in the artist's efforts as well as in the work, and appreciation must emulate these efforts in order to have access to the insights that novel works contain. But this emulation contrasts taste in that it is more in the nature of an uncovering than an assessment, and what is uncovered is the content of artistic expression. This content combines a unique image of the world with a record of the creating process. The requirement now given to appreciation is that it emulate the process in order to understand the image—a vicarious creativity, as it were, that succeeds as appreciation by pushing aside the aloofness that beauty requires of taste.

These considerations extend well beyond Kant's aesthetic theory, for they signal a later context of theory in which beauty is rejected as an aesthetic value. In this context, artworks that maintain their dependence on the "disinterested" appreciation of natural beauty come to be seen as promulgating a worldview that is conventional and conservative—not at all the view of genius. In this new climate, appreciation must contend not only with the implications of the historical evolution of style in art but with problems coming from its other flank: artistic creativity. Here, the pressure on the concept of taste is exerted by the need for it to cope with, not only the products, but the actions of the artist. Kant, although he gives a functional account of artistic activity, shows no psychological or social curiosity, and he includes that account within his discussion of sublimity. This suggests that artistic activity, like the storm at sea, is a force of nature whose philosophical importance is best viewed from a distance. Perhaps Kant felt that this distance is needed for the view that so eccentric a human activity is also a theoretical conduit between noumena and phenomena, the view that artistic spontaneity is nature's way of revealing its form in artifacts. However that may be, Kant did not address the possibility of using artistic creativity as a model for social and moral behavior.

Hegel was little better than Kant in this regard, for although his artists are firmly placed in the dynamics of history, they remain types, philosophical instruments for the symbolization of change, meriting attention only if, in their extraordinary capacity as genius, their works are historically predictive. The correlation between creativity and general human consciousness points, rather, to the aesthetics of Schopenhauer. Artistic expression, here, is revelatory in a different way: It does not exemplify in the formal sense, nor does it anticipate in the teleological sense; rather, it *uncovers* the reality that underlies—and is masked by—change.

In Part I, I show that both Hegel and Schopenhauer reject Kant's stricture on noumenal knowledge. For Hegel, such knowledge is possible as a teleological endpoint: the fulfillment of spirit's evolution. For Schopenhauer, on the other hand, it is immediately available—but only to those who risk penetrating the conventional substitutes for such knowledge. Artistic activity, the creative or "expressive" act, embodies this risk; and the artist, as an individual existent, exemplifies the dubious consequences of success.

For both Kant and Hegel, the philosophical value of art is located primarily in the artwork and its appeciation, for it is there that the epistemic transfer takes place. Schopenhauer separates appreciation from both taste and history and locates it, rather, in the sympathetic emulation of artistic creativity. It is through such emulation that epistemic access to the noumenon is gained, and as a consequence, the meanings of artworks are revealed.

FIVE

Schopenhauer and Expression

1. TASTE AND CREATIVITY

FOR THE nineteenth-century aesthetic theory that gives primary importance to the creative process and thereby introduces psychological values into aesthetics, I return to Schopenhauer. His account contains philosophical reasons for the antagonism between taste and creativity that Kant's theory implies but does not develop. These reasons have to do with the way Schopenhauer conceives of art's special epistemic function. For Kant, art provides a semblance of order that permits *us* to impute that order to nature. Schopenhauer's conception is more ambitious: Art is a source of knowledge; its multiple images show us what the noumenal world is like by presenting the will in its "adequate objectivity." These images, in contrast to their role in Kant's aesthetics, are at cross-purposes with our empirical and practical representations of the world. Schopenhauer states: "Every work of art really endeavors to show us life and things as they are in reality, but these cannot be grasped directly by everyone through the mist of objective and subjective contingencies. Art takes away this mist."[1] For Kant, artworks intimate; for Schopenhauer they reveal. The Kantian hope is that artworks corroborate the assumptions of empirical knowledge and moral action; Schopenhauer, to the contrary, sees artworks as revealing the delusions upon which such knowledge and actions are based.

If we take appreciation—the exercise of taste—to be compatible with our conventional world through the support it gives to our ideals for that world's perfectibility, we are in the Kantian framework: The artistic image of a noumenal rationality encourages us to act as if our ideals can be realized—whether or not that image is veridical or our actions successful. Schopenhauer's concept of art's access to the noumenal world is quite different: The images that artworks provide *are* veridical, but what they show mocks our ideals and denigrates our actions. This knowledge is at odds with the conventional beliefs that pass for collective wisdom, and it leaves us with no recourse but an individual solitary passivity. The intimations of noumenal rationality in the Kantian reflective judgment provide, at least, hope of a convergence between human action and rational grounds. Schopenhauer's noumenon has no such grounds to provide; its imperative is of action, and rationality must find its place in the reactive uniquely human stance of nonaction. This stance is not collectively viable, for the interactions of groups, however justified, are nonetheless actions and, thus, determined by the will. The solitary stance that supports rationality—Schopenhauer's moral stance—has no grounds for either hope or expectation that others will adopt it.

This reveals a fundamental difference in the function of taste in the two aesthetics. A taste that recommends itself to the collective—a taste that is, in Kant's terms, "necessary and universal"—is, for Schopenhauer, a duplicitous instrument.[2] Such taste exhibits all the mendacities of social collectives: It ascribes order and purpose to its subject, its own history, through the structures it erects and justifies, and it thereby masks the true, aggressive and appetitive, nature of social interaction. Here Schopenhauer inverts Kant's aesthetic: If the central value in aesthetics is taste, and if this, in turn, is governed by the expectation that "harmony in appearances" is a sign of noumenal rationality, it results in a deceit. It tells us nothing of the world behind appearances but merely shows us the appearances we prefer—those which assure us through their formal presentations that nature actually is as we would wish it to be. For Schopenhauer, nature's reality is precisely the opposite of our wishes, and he gives the aesthetic the task of finding this out.

2. THE FUNCTION OF ART

Although Schopenhauer rejects the Kantian linkage between the images of art and a rationally based ontology, he nevertheless goes further than Kant in schematizing and categorizing the various ways in which artworks present the images—the "objectifications"—of his irrational, or, better, "nonrational," noumenon.[3] In Schopenhauer's theory, art's contribution to ontology consists in its ability to symbolize, according to the referential capacities of each medium, the different "grades" of the instantiations of the will. It is the descriptive function of art that is at issue here, and Schopenhauer distinguishes the "adequate objectifications" of artistic images from our ordinary, empirical or practical, accounts of the world. Artworks present "true" pictures of things in the world by showing them as they are when freed of our "willful" uses of them. In this endeavor, the various forms of art correlate with different aspects of their subject, and these differences turn out to be normative as well as descriptive. Schopenhauer establishes a correspondence between his categories of art and his analysis of the manner in which the workings of the will are revealed in nature. The most primitive of these instantiations is geologic, the formations of rock and earth; correspondingly, the "lowest" art form is architecture, whose works are subject to the same structural forces, inertia, gravity, et cetera, that govern the slow pace of geologic change. The visual arts are higher on this scale, primarily because they are freer from the physical forces that control their subjects, and thus, their representations can be presented illusionistically. In keeping with his emphasis on content, Schopenhauer distinguishes between works of visual art on the basis of subject rather than style. Representations of natural forms are therefore lower on the scale than human likenesses. Literature is given the next highest level, on the presumption that verbal descriptions are free of the extensional limitations of visual depictions. The symbolic limits of pictorial illusion are seen as narrower than the range of literary fiction, the metaphors of the former effectively limited by their immediacy, those of the latter open to development in time. But the differential in content, whether description or depiction, is the same for both arts: Empires in turmoil are more fitting as representational subjects than are individual psyches and their troubles. This latter subject becomes the content of another, higher art.

Schopenhauer reserves the highest level of artistic achievement for music. From one standpoint of his theory, music remains representational: In its harmonic structure, it proceeds from the supporting bass voice, across the mediations of alto and tenor, to the soprano's power of melody. Through this progression, it symbolizes the entire range of the will's instantiations—from geologic forms to human actions. From another standpoint, however, these interweavings of harmonic voices also capture the gradations of the will as they are manifest in our psychic processes—from inchoate longings, through daily copings, to articulated ideals. By so bringing the "outer" and "inner" worlds together through the agency of music, Schopenhauer presents a thesis that is crucial for his entire theory: He links the dynamics of natural forms, the organic world, with the dynamics of sentience, the world of feelings. In this way, Schopenhauer's noumenon, "will," is shown to underlie both physical and psychological realities, and the arts function to bridge the two. The visual and literary arts are limited by the indirect nature of their symbols; the temporal relationship between description and event is fictional rather than actual. This relationship becomes actual in music, for Schopenhauer considers music to be a direct analogue of the will rather than a representation, however adequate, of its objectifications. Music alone presents the will in its immediacy: by symbolizing it as it is in action and by correlating its action with the action of our psyches. Appreciation, under this theory, consists of experiencing the parallelism between the two forms of action and, thus, of coming to know the metaphysical source of subjectivity. This is a stronger epistemic claim for art than is made by either Kant or Hegel. The appreciation of art, in Schopenhauer's terms, provides direct knowledge of the reality that underlies both our descriptions of the world and our self-awareness. It thus confirms what the contemplative stance also teaches—that the reachings of subjectivity lead nowhere, and desire is never fulfilled.

The passivity and disengagement that Schopenhauer affirms as the only proper moral response to the will has a certain similarity to Kant's requirement of disinterestedness: Both reject pragmatics and immediacy in favor of aloofness and distance. But there are important differences: Kant brings this, rationally determined, attitude *to* appreciation as the key to beauty's significations. Schopenhauer's stance is the *consequence* of appreciation, the psyche "burnt out" in its efforts at piercing the veil of illusion. Kant uses disinterestedness to signify an interest that is free of desire. This purified interest then has a chance of estimating beauty on its own terms, that is, "formally," and there finding the wanted support for morality. This is, in effect, a rational purification of imagination, a wrought distinction between intrinsic form and extrinsic uses. Schopenhauer also needs such a disengagement for both the appreciation of art and the moral stance. But his way of achieving it is quite opposite: His entails a quintessentially romantic "going through" willed experience until exhaustion permits the needed insight. Schopenhauer writes: "Only in a few is mere knowledge sufficient to bring about the denial of the will . . . in most cases the will must be broken by the greatest personal suffering before its self-denial appears."[4] Kant's aesthetic appreciation looks for rationality in nature; Schopenhauer's follows through and past nature, into the rationality that opposes it. Appreciation's guide in this journey is the artist.

3. ARTISTIC EXPRESSION

Schopenhauer's thesis that noumenal reality is knowable exacts a somewhat unphilosophical price from one of its epistemic instruments. Although artistic creativity reveals the thing-in-itself, artists do not benefit from this revelation; somewhat perversely, their ability in this regard is at the expense of happiness, even survival. To some extent, the costs that artists incur for their efforts can be traced to some of Schopenhauer's philosophical excesses: There is, for example, his replacement of Kant's reflection on a possible harmony between knowledge and nature with the assertion that the relationship is, in fact, knowable but is one of disharmony. And there is his denial that there is any purpose, direction, or goal to the activities of the will—in effect, a rejection of teleology as either a Kantian "hope" or a Hegelian "fact." In the realm of theory, the manner in which these costs are paid is a matter of how one reads the later history of philosophy. At a subsequent point in this study, I discuss the influence of Schopenhauer's descriptions of the creative process on the doctrines and the art of modernism. Here, I use his theory to make the transition from the metaphysical description of the processes of the will to the more strictly aesthetic accounts of artistic creativity: creativity as "expression."

This evocation of expression must be qualified, however. Schopenhauer's aesthetics, as I indicate in Chapter Two, is not an expression theory. For him, art remains an epistemic tool, and artistic process is valued for its adequacy in forming this tool. In this, he differs from such overtly Romantic contemporaries as Schelling and Schiller. Nevertheless, the concept of expression is to be found in his theories, and its role there is crucial, as I see it, to later theories of that kind. For Schopenhauer, the will "expresses itself" through the conflict between process and its instantiations. This conflict—between primal insatiability and its conventional satisfactions—is not a routine albeit cosmological affair, and its symbolic replication through art is not a simple chronicling of the conflict. Expression and its product remain divided in both art and the creative process. Music, which Schopenhauer places at the apogee of the arts, avoids the will's efforts at self-instantiation by taking the pure form of the process as its subject. On the other side, artists must emulate the insatiability of the will in seeking their images, but the images they reach defy the will by showing its antithesis—the Platonic idea. Philosophers also seek the antithesis of the will, for this constitutes philosophical knowledge; but having reached it, they can rest with the achievement.

Artists, on the other hand, are constrained to project this quiescence through the images of art, and the journey to the surface must be retraced. So the artist, like the will, is conflicted between process and instantiation, and in this conflict lies artistic expression. For Schopenhauer, as I have indicated, the content, and point, of this expression is external to the artist; it concerns the nature of reality. In later theory, this reality turns inward and becomes the search for the essential, nonconventional self. Through this transition, self-expression inherits the value Schopenhauer places on aesthetic knowledge of the will as thing-in-itself.

Schopenhauer's way of describing the nature of artistic activity and its effect upon the artist can be cast into an informal syllogism: Artists express their experiences of the world through their artworks, and since these expressions expose a reality that has been suppressed by conventional beliefs about the world, they also attack these beliefs. Thus, these expressions come not to be accepted as fit subjects for aesthetic appreciation, and, often together with their authors, they are rejected by the societies in which they were created. The "exemplary" artist of the eighteenth-century Enlightenment here becomes the "misunderstood" artist of nineteenth-century Romanticism.[5] In this latter guise, however, artists lose the protective neutrality of their Kantian role as conduits for nature's, essentially benevolent, voice. Instead, they bear the onus placed on those who understand that voice to be malevolent and who yet insist on bringing its message to the rest of us. This special understanding, formerly the task of appreciation, now devolves upon the artist. In this context, artworks, are no longer symbolic versions of nature's beauties given us for disinterested contemplation. They are, instead, interpretations that momentarily separate nature from its principle of strife and thereby admonish us to separate ourselves from it as well, so that these "selves" can become the subjects of our disinterested contemplation. This changes the nature of appreciation and diminishes its philosophical importance in comparison to creativity. The audience is no longer in the Kantian position of directing sensibility at art and nature so as to generate philosophical meaning. The artist does that for them, and the capacity to do so is Schopenhauer's version of Kant's "genius." Here, I call this capacity "expression."

The world and all its processes, in Schopenhauer's philosophy, are instantiations of the will. If we would wish to personalize this principle (and, indeed, Schopenhauer's linguistic dramatics encourage this), we could say that the will "expresses itself" through these instantiations. We, as things in the world, are among its expressions, and we confirm this through our own expressions, which, in ordinary terms, we equate with all the actions of our lives. Given this sense of inclusion, there would seem to be no distinction, except in scope, between individual expression and the workings of the will. But, for Schopenhauer, the will is both a noumenon and an antagonist. As such, it is incomplete. So there is, in this theory, an expression that cannot be attributed to the will, namely, that through which we characterize it as it really is by showing what it is not: the expression of art. The reality that art reveals is "will-less" and therefore cannot be subsumed under, because it is antithetical to, what the will expresses. Artistic expression points to a possibility beyond the will and, thus, establishes the metaphysical paradox of extending reality beyond the limits of its noumenal identity. This effort at emancipating image from process, idea from will, serves the cause of philosophical autonomy in the dualistic sense that it separates rationality from nature. The consequences of this move for my limited topic are these: Through its separation of the two expressions, noumenal and artistic, Schopenhauer's theory anticipates the historical rift, characteristic of Romanticism and early modernism, between the creation of art and social expectations. The gap, for Schopenhauer, between reality and our representations is not epistemic but normative, for the difficulty lies not in knowing what is real but in our collective preferences for illusion. Artistic expression is given the role of countering the expressions of the will, and shares with philosophy the critical task of exposing the varieties of social illusion. The relation between art and its social context, now charactized by this opposition between the will's function and its artistic imaging, extends this opposition to the images' source and strips the artist of the protection afforded by the essentially benign Kantian role of "nature's voice." This role is replaced by the new role of social marginality that becomes the dominant characterization of creativity in the nineteenth and early twentieth centuries.

In this context of opposition between art and will, the artist's task is to produce works that show the unchanging negativity of a reality that we, collectively, would rather not know. Appreciation, here, is given a diminished theoretical role. Art's audience, having neither the capacity nor the courage to reach these revelations on their own, must now take them secondhand from the artist.[6] The role of nature as aesthetic subject is also diminished. What adequate appreciation comes to under this thesis is an individual willingness to reject the tasteful enjoyments of nature perceived as harmonious, for the painful truth of the antagonistic nature exposed by art. Here, the consequences of this rift between artistic expression and audience expectations first show themselves: The artist, like the philosopher, seeks noumenal knowledge; but its pursuit through art, although philosophically vital, is destructive to its agent. The difficulties, the psychic disorders, poverty, alienation, that beset artists are but evidence of the destructive nature of the will in the guise of social disfavor. In his descriptions of artists' difficulties in coping with the conditions of life, Schopenhauer presents an early posit of the affinities between artistic expression and mental instability: "Men of genius are often subject to violent emotions and irrational passions . . . and, in general, may exhibit several weaknesses that are closely akin to madness."[7]

Nevertheless, the justification for art, given its effects and the nature of its message, remains metaphysical for Schopenhauer. His artists are much like the saints of early Christianity, those who could see the Devil and would wrestle with him—whatever the consequences. To extend this metaphor: Despite Schopenhauer's self-professed atheism, his construal of "will" has always seemed to me somewhat demonic. The insatiable aggression, the ceaseless action that never leads to satisfaction, the constant need for duplicity, seem aptly to characterize the fallen Lucifer. Also, Schopenhauer's philosophical remedy, the withdrawal from action and the abnegation of desire, has aspects of the Christian ascetic response. Schopenhauer gives the artist the overweening task of revealing the truth, the noumenon as irrational force, so that the rest of us can recognize it in our lives and escape it. The images of art facilitate the task of moral inquiry by convincing us that the quietism of contemplation is the only moral course. But the artist, faithful to the imperatives of creativity, cannot take advantage of that course: The artist "is captivated by a consideration of the spectacle of the will's objectification. . . . Meanwhile, he himself bears the cost of producing that play; in other words, he himself is the will objectifying itself and remaining in constant suffering. That pure, true, and profound knowledge of the inner nature of the world now becomes for him an end in itself."[8]

4. THE VALUE OF ART

We are accustomed, these days, not only to the psychological linkage of artistic expression with the notion of "neurosis" but to its formal linkage with the notion of "distortion." It is a commonplace that artists distort reality in order to show us their subjective reactions to it and that we find aesthetic value in the unexpected variations of such subjectivity. But this is not what Schopenhauer has in mind. He considers the will to be the common ground of both natural and psychological processes. The images that artists present us, therefore, he would consider not as distortions but as revelations of reality, the best revelations we have.

Schopenhauer's description of the referential nature of artworks through the model of the Platonic Forms does not signal an agreement between aesthetic theories. Plato considers art's images to be reality "thrice removed," not merely shadows on the cave wall but the shadows of those shadows.[9] However, Schopenhauer rejects the Platonic thesis that artistic images are but poor imitations of things and, thus, epistemically misleading. Instead, he holds that artworks directly represent the Forms, indicating by this that art presents images of things as they are when free of participation in the processes of the will. Thus, in Schopenhauer's aesthetics, things "as they are in themselves" are so when free of the "thing-in-itself"—the noumenal will. Even music, which, unlike the other arts, directly images the will as process, presents it as a "temporal essence" and thus, paradoxically, frees this process from itself.

In the *Phaedrus,* Plato describes the gods as driving their chariots, replete with matching steeds, into that "region beyond the heavens" where they may glimpse "the eternal forms." Ordinary mortals, with their ill-matched and contentious steeds, cannot reach the vantage needed for that glimpse. This metaphor of a journey readily adapts to Schopenhauer's construal of the creative process, with the difference, however, that, although they may exceed ordinary mortals in their capacity to perceive essences, artists are not gods. Given the well-known dislike that Greek gods have for the "hubris" of human ambition, one could carry this metaphor further and speculate that artists' misfortunes are, in fact, penalties exacted by those gods for the overreaching insights of creativity. Such a metaphor may even be practically useful in redirecting society's need to cast blame, and in helping assuage its guilt, by thus enlisting the gods—through, perhaps, psychoanalytic theory—into serving as an antidote for the most dire of Schopenhauer's conclusions about the artist's life. However, when hubris is recast as neurosis, then its alleviation, not the exacting of penalties, is the proper response. Through this shift, creativity's philosophical role begins to diminish.

By restricting noumenal knowledge to the gods, and thereby placing a limitation on human epistemic capacity, Plato is much like Kant. Schopenhauer, a more thoroughgoing idealist, accepts no such limitation and makes his noumenon accessible to artists, but at the cost that they, qua artists, remain captives of the will's process while knowing it as essence. It is a difficult position to maintain, but to do otherwise would be—"at last tired of this play, [to] lay hold on the real"—to become a philosopher.[10]

The philosophical, if not social, instability that Schopenhauer assigns the artistic vocation eventually diminishes together with the interest in its primary subject. Will is too eccentric a noumenon for sustained philosophical or artistic attention, and in the later history of this theme, human willing, its origins and value, becomes the new subject of art. It then becomes evident that artists need not defy the noumenal will to justify their vocation; self-expression is hard enough. But Schopenhauer's concern with artistic process had a lasting impact on aesthetic theory: It established expression as the competitor of taste for the designation of primary aesthetic value, and it marked the transition from Enlightenment spectator aesthetics to the concerns with creativity of Romanticism. As this theme moved further into the modern era, it functioned as a social as well as aesthetic demarcator: Conservative versus radical in social theory came to equate with academic versus avant-garde in the arts. Contrary to Schopenhauer's insistence that human strife is actually capitulation to the will and therefore meaningless, these ideological conflicts increased in tempo throughout the nineteenth-century and into the modern era. Much of the impetus for that acceleration, and the increase in vehemence, can be attributed to another theory: the Hegelian theory of "evolution of spirit" in its version as "progress in art."

SIX

Hegel and Progress

1. TRUTH AND ART

HEGEL'S own assessment of his theories has a romantic flamboyance that is often at odds with some philosophical scruples of the present day: He calls his theorizing "science," yet takes care to disassociate it, as being of a more comprehensive and thus "higher" sort, from the physical sciences. He also makes no strong distinctions between empirical assertions, moral laws, and aesthetic symbols, and he assigns each of them the task of contributing, in its way, to the all-encompassing determinations that are philosophical truths.[1] It is in Hegel, more unequivocally than in either Kant or Schopenhauer, that the claim is made that art is truth bearing; but this is in keeping with his general theory, in which the term is so broadly applied as to give all symbolic activities a part in its determination.

Hegel's concern with truth is not primarily to distinguish it from falsity or ambiguity, but to judge its comprehensiveness—how much of the world it reveals. In this sense, there is no statement that is entirely false, nor is there a symbol of any kind that is not concerned with truth: Falsity reveals that which it denies, and the most abstruse conceit can be traced to an originary concretion. For Hegel, both the comprehensiveness and the particular form of truth depend on the historical position of its symbol. Not only are there differences as to what "being true" comes to at various historical times, but times differ according to the forms in which truth finds its best presentations. This dependency of truth on history marks truth's dependency, as well, upon the principle through which Hegel gives history its own form, that is, the teleological form of "progress." On this score, Hegel writes: "World history is the manifestation of the Divine, the absolute process of Spirit in its highest forms. It is this development wherein it achieves its truth and the consciousness of itself. The products of its stages are the world-historical national spirits . . . their art, religion, science."[2]

The notion that art progresses is more familiar to us than the notion that truth progresses. But this first familiarity is tied to a recent period in art history where value claims include the notion of a work's instantiation of progress. Truth, on the other hand, is not so easily relativized to style. Despite recurrent philosophical hesitations about the basis, transitivity, or importance of truth, we think of its history as one of diminishing error. Unlike art, it has no independent stylistic virtues that might historically sustain it despite, or as, error. But Hegel does not accept the aesthetic distinction between stylistic value and truth, for he locates art among such other truth-bearing symbols as religion and philosophy, and he includes the capacity for truth among his criteria for evaluating art, (see Chapter Three). On this account, art's progress is a function of its capacity to symbolize the progressive nature of historical change, the progress of truth, within the limits of its own time and symbolic form. But the cultural relativity implied by this thesis is secondary to the absolute of history's grand unfolding: "Change" is a "working out" of what, so far, remains covert. To simply say, for example, that art "is true to" or, more circumspectly, "mirrors" its time is not strong enough for Hegel. Progress in history needs potent symbols that both document its particular stages and place these documents within a metacultural account of historical change and direction.

Hegel, being (historically) free of present-day scruples, identifies this account with his own philosophy, and he gives art a significant place within it.

2. OBJECTIONS

Before I look further at this aesthetic juncture of "truth" and "progress," and at its interesting ramifications for later aesthetic theory, I want briefly to indicate some general terms of the argument against such theories as Hegel's. This argument is largely associated with contemporary Anglo-American philosophy, and it helps an understanding of Hegel to contrast the holistic ambitions of nineteenth-century speculative philosophy with the specializations and modesties of present-day theories. The contrast also provides some insights into the very different views, across the two centuries, about the value and uses of art.

It is not a present practice, especially within the analytic tradition, to think of artworks as epistemically viable, to consider them as *providers* of knowledge. Rather, in the main, artworks are seen as nonassertorial symbols that function mainly to give us a certain kind of, aesthetic, pleasure. While such symbols might be taken as *sources* of knowledge, as evidence for the veridical statements we make about artworks, about their style, origins, value, et cetera, yet, in what they themselves say or show, they are neither true nor false. Although it may be that some artworks, through the mimetic credibility of what they say or show, seem to refer to the world, these references cannot be taken as denotative, as providing us with "facts." Under this construal, descriptions in novels, representations in paintings, musical or poetic expressions, all belong to the realm of fictions. And fiction, if we follow Plato's beliefs, can be misleading in a world dependent on fact.

Yet it does seem that, even when we grant these restrictions, we cannot conclude that art tells us *nothing* about the world. Appreciation, after all, is not delusion. So we also grant a world, or worlds, of the imagination, those fictional worlds we reconstruct out of the actual one, which enable us to better enjoy, cope with, enrich, the world we live in. But these interactions are often restricted by their referral to the domain of pleasure; and such pleasure, even if of a distinctly aesthetic sort, is not to be confused with knowlege. Thus, the modern wisdom, by and large, does not permit art to help us better understand the world; it maintains a closed border between the many worlds of art and our single real one.[3]

3. COMPARISONS

While this distinction between symbols that are truth bearing and those that are aesthetic is characteristic of many modern epistemological theories, it is a recurring theme, given Plato's assist, in the history of philosophy. The period here in question, German philosophy of the late eighteenth and nineteenth centuries, is actually atypical in its move to grant aesthetics an epistemic function. Here, the distinction loses its univocal character and becomes a matter of fitting symbol types to the various judgments required by a comprehensive system. Kant, for example, first distinguishes between the criteria for empirical assertions and moral imperatives, and shows that judgments of beauty and art are not demonstrable through either set of criteria. He then undertakes a semantic ascent and proceeds to link the empirical and moral realms through the aesthetic, through beauty as it is generated by the "free play of the imagination." Kant thus assigns an epistemic function to aesthetic judgments, in that, although they themselves are neither true nor false, they support our commitment to the truth of these other, empirical and ethical, judgments.

Because neither Hegel nor Schopenhauer locate truth exclusively within verbal and logical propositions, they are more willing than Kant to extend epistemic authority to the aesthetic; but the results of this extension are quite different in each case. Within Schopenhauer's dualistic theory, truth is not a unified concept. "Will" and "idea" refer to different realities. How we know these realities, and what we know through them, cannot be brought together within a single description. Here, the term "reality" only occasionally accepts the modifier "empirical," and so it happens that some entities we can truly know, such as those which form the content of artworks, are nonempirical. Accordingly, for Schopenhauer, artistic truth is a form of truth, for it gives an adequate account of its subject, the will, which is both real and nonempirical. Ontological commitment to this subject follows the Platonic model by identifying the will as the "underlying" reality upon which the empirical is constructed. Justification of *this* thesis, however, is left to introspection, to the evidence our feelings provide.

Reality, for Hegel, is a unity, and thus, "truth" is a holistic concept. But as his reality is also a process, one of spirit's self-actualization in time, any particular instance of truth is partial. Hegel's truth holism goes beyond uniform applicability to matters of fact; it applies equally to moral and aesthetic judgments and even to its supposed contradictories.[4] Under this construal, there is no such thing as absolute error—as "pure negativity." All error contains an element of the truth through which it is seen as error, in the same way that all indeterminacy contains a sign of the determinate through which, in the first place, it can be discriminated. By the same token, truth is partial because, in any instance of assertion, something is as yet unknowable and thus cannot be asserted. Still, the statement that there are such unknowables is itself true, and it also provides the impetus to expand the range of truth. One such expansion occurs when the reexamination of what is false identifies grounds for rescuing it from exclusion, for bringing (some of) it back into the argument. The other occurs when indeterminacy becomes "something indeterminate," through a perhaps inadvertant extension of an argument, and, as a something, becomes an epistemic compliant. The process whereby subjects of knowledge that are only abstractly cognizable become determinate and, thus, actually knowable makes truth itself subject to teleology. The capacity of truth progresses as does its subject. Hegel identifies the goal of this process as "absolute" knowledge, a seamless ideal whose historical anticipations take the different forms of science, art, religion, philosophy. Each such form is limited in range and in what counts as its subject, although the internal history of each form is the progressive expansion of its subject. Each expansion has its limits, however, and truth's symbolic forms succeed each other in the struggle to remain adequate to the increasing comprehensiveness of their common subject.

4. ART AND PROGRESS

The much discussed notion of the "end of art," the notion that art, at some point, becomes historically irrelevant, derives from this Hegelian thesis of the symbolic evolution of truth.[5] The actual practices of art are not at issue here: Art's end is an epistemic death; irrelevance does not entail that the activity disappear from the world. In Hegel's categorization of the arts, the last and highest form is poetry, the art of discourse. The achievements of poetry also mark its perilous similarity to another mode of discourse, the philosophical; and the forays of poetry into that, for it, inhospitable, content signify, at the same time, its highest ambitions and its failure.

There is another notion, also prophetic, that contributes to this scenario. Hegel remarks that the late stages of art are marked by the propensity, in appreciation, to substitute a self-conscious analysis for direct aesthetic enjoyment.[6] The end of art, then, seems to generate two kinds of aesthetically (and, thus, philosophically) irrelevant chatter—by art and about art. Both are inadequate for the same reasons: Art's proper truth, as Hegel tells us, is "the pure appearance of the Idea to sense."[7] If this is so, then that art which presumes to tell us, with an unwarranted and intrusive intimacy, about itself undermines its purity; and we who need that talk as a focus for appreciation cannot properly grasp art's appearance. Yet, all this inadequacy is also a kind of high point; it is, after all, the end of the best that art can do for spirit's elucidation.

It is curious that this notion of the end of art continues to intrigue us: We talk about it as if the end that Hegel alluded to over a century ago had been put off for today. Maybe there is more than one reason, or one occasion, for art to end. Hegel puts his sense of it this way: "But if it is a matter of the consciousness of *truth*, then the *beauty* of the appearance, and the representation, is an accessory and rather indifferent, for the truth is present for consciousness independently of art."[8] Art relinquishes beauty, then, for the sake of truth because, in "these" skewed times—and which times, in comparison to some ideal past, are not skewed?—truth must become free of beauty in order to be heard. It seems then that, for Hegel, the disappearance of the *possibility* of beauty from art constitutes art's demise. But Hegel did not foresee the advent of modernism, and so he did not conceive of an art for which *freedom from* beauty (to be sure, the beauty of nineteenth-century academicism) was a signpost of its own truth and of its continuing historical importance.

In the history of aesthetics after Hegel, the interdependency between beauty and aesthetic truth is severed. The irrelevance of beauty for art becomes central to those doctrines that, by following Hegel's telic line of theory, interpret later, modern, art through the conflict between its own formal progress and the cultural stasis exemplified, in part, by a decadent adherence to beauty. In this setting, the truth content of art functions as criticism of society's unwillingness to accept and, presumably, benefit from these newly unfettered symbols of aesthetic truth. I note here that both for Hegel and for later social theorists, "unwillingness," with its implication of willful rejection, is more historically reprehensible than is "incapacity," which is simply rejection by omission or ignorance.

5. HEGEL'S TASTES IN ART

Hegel could not have known that his death was to coincide with the beginnings of modern art. He lived in a Germany that, in short order, was faced with a number of political and social upheavals: First came the ideological ferment of the French Revolution, and then its grim constriction through the subsequent "Terror." This was followed by Napolean—the quintessential Hegelian "world-historical individual"—who reestablished order and empire only to dislocate its promise through an invasion of Hegel's Germany. This sequence of raised and shattered hopes may bear on the fact that, despite the radical implications of his theories, Hegel's own political stance, particularly after the battle of Jena, became more cautious and conservative.[9]

In a parallel sense, Hegel's attitude toward the contemporary art of his time was also cautious, perhaps even aloof. Romanticism in music peaked in early nineteenth-century Germany; yet, in the *Aesthetics,* Hegel traces musical value from his idol, Mozart, to Rossini; there is only oblique negative reference to Beethoven.[10] Although he writes at length on music's capacity to explore subjective feeling, he is ill at ease with purely instrumental music, music without a text. On that point he writes: "Especially in recent times, music has torn itself from a content already clear on its own account and retreated in this way into its own medium. . . . bare interest in the purely musical elements of the composition . . . scarcely appeals to the general human interest in art."[11] In the visual arts, Hegel places his highest value on the Raphaels and Correggios of Renaissance Italy, but he does not cross contemporary boundaries into, for example, the France of David, Ingres, and Delacroix. Here, too, he suggests a dependency of painting on literature, and seems to fix painting's role as the portrayal of human character, often literary characters. He closes his section on that art with the remark that artists of his day "know neither what man and human color is nor what the forms are in which man expresses that he is man in fact."[12] This remark could be read, in a perverse way, as an anticipation of Impressionism. However, Hegel does not indicate that all art has reached its developmental end. Although the great achievements of painting and music may be in his historical past, literature, in the persons of Klopstock, Schiller, and, especially, Goethe, continues on as a potent symbol. Here, Hegel traces a normative constant from Greek drama, through Shakespeare, into his own time.[13]

Hegel's tastes in art, as is also true of Kant and Schopenhauer, are nothing if not philosophical; that is, they (must) elucidate his conceptual system of the arts. Given Hegel's tastes, then, it would seem that he places himself at the historical point of his own systemic description, in which painting and music have already given way to poetry as viable symbols of spirit's historical course. It is not therefore a matter of (mere) taste but of historical inevitability—process normatively instantiated—that music and painting of his time is not as "good" as the literature. Art is not quite dead, for poetry still enjoys its apogee in his present.

But there is another side to Hegel's view of historical progress, one that casts doubt on this particular corroboration of developmental stages through judgments of taste. Hegel writes: "Historical change, seen abstractly, has long been understood generally as involving a progress toward the better, the more perfect. . . . Actually, perfectibility is something almost as undetermined as mutability in general; it is without aim and purpose and without a standard of change. The better, the more perfect to which it is supposed to attain, is entirely undetermined."[14] So it would seem that Hegel's assessments of the art of his time do not take into account his own sense of historical process: They do not include the possibility that art would force a change in the *terms* of its threatened historical demise—that, for example, painting, in self-defense, would appropriate the temporality of music or the conceptuality of poetry. This lacuna evokes the peculiarly un-Hegelian circumstance in which art's self-consciousness, its view of its historical self, cannot contribute to the course of its future. This is a dualistic but nondialectical Hegel: the inevitability of *an sich* without the freedom of *für-sich*.[15] The ideologies of modernism that build on Hegel reject this view and, in doing so, provide appreciation with a new content: Art faces its historical inadequacy as a truth-bearing symbol by decreasing the, formal and conceptual, distance between itself and historically ascendant symbols. Painting does become more like music, and art as a whole becomes more like theory.[16] Here, one remembers Hegel's admonition that poetry, in its late stages, is in danger of emulating philosophy. This can be taken as another (unwitting) anticipation of modernism. Late art encourages, even includes as its proper part, talk about itself; and that talk has generally to do with aesthetic alternatives to art's loss of immediacy—its inability to any longer present its truth solely and completely through the gratifications of beauty. As I note above, Hegel takes late art's seductiveness for theory to be a weakness, a doomed infatuation with symbolic forms of another, higher, order. And recognizing this weakness encourages appreciation to follow spirit's truth away from art into the more rarified realms of religion and philosophy. Hegel's alignment of beauty with art of the past seeks the reassurance of history that the future will remain rational. Kant also needs such reassurance, but he looks for it primarily in the aesthetics of nature. Schopenhauer cannot be so reassured.

The schism between art and beauty is also a schism between art and reason. Beauty, for Hegel, is reason's self-demonstration, and art retains philosophical value only during that time when *artistic* beauty can be its primary content. There are other beauties for Hegel, for example, beauty of the soul and of the reconciliation of opposites. But it is only sensual beauty that is proper to art. And with its historical exhaustion, art no longer has philosophical importance. At this historical moment of schism between art and reason, in which his own theories are implicated, Hegel does not attempt a dialectical rescue of art; he does not suggest that we "overcome" this deficiency in content by denying that the characteristic of beauty is a necessary condition for appreciation. Hegel does not, in sum, consider that art might, yet again, transcend its content and appropriate one that provides appreciation with a subject other than that offered by the sense of beauty. It seems likely that Hegel's primary reason for leaving art in the historical lurch was, what we today would call, the categorical rigidity in his system: When one symbolic form fulfills its telic mission, we must move to its successor. In this regard, *Aufhebung* seems more an autocratic than democratic principle, for it works better through the supplantation of forms than through their internal capacity for transformation.

There may be another reason for Hegel's willingness to circumscribe the possibilities of art, and this is a belief that to change the conditions of appreciation would support, perhaps even instigate, the disruption of social cohesiveness. This explanation would give Hegel's antipathy to the more radical art of his time a social as well as theoretical basis. It could be argued that replacing beauty with another aesthetic content would deny the appreciation that is specific to beauty—sensitivity to harmony, nuance, equilibrium, subordination—its role in preserving a society based on certain distinctions of class and birthright. The correlation here between appreciative capacity and social status indicates that the values of the former can be used to justify the continuation of the latter. On the same view, an appreciation indifferent to such values could be enlisted to support an art that, through a different formal instantiation, is hostile to these wanted social distinctions. The alliance between new art and radical social values would thus be forged. But this, of course, is precisely the characteristic alliance of modernism. The ideologies that support this alliance, both the art and its critical implications, are Hegelian in that the common value is "progress." These ideologies depart from Hegel, however, by affirming that art, like other social forms, can emancipate itself from its own definition and, thus, continue as a telic symbol.[17]

6. TOWARD MODERNISM

In discussing the Symbolic art form, Hegel attributes the "grotesqueness" of its imagery to the effort at depicting in art what is not (yet) possible in conception. The appreciation, there, of what is not (yet) beautiful, and thus barely true, is anticipatory; it awaits its emending in history, in Classical art, and this eventuality (at least in hindsight) justifies the early practice. In late art, however, the "second separation" between truth and beauty cannot be emended because it occurs *after* the achievement of their synthesis. As there is nothing further between them to anticipate, there are no good philosophical reasons to justify appreciating the artistic "residue" of this second separation. This is the Hegelian thesis that art ends because truth no longer requires a sensuous image. The thesis also implies that appreciation at this point, when directed at new art, becomes trivialized.

It may be that Hegel saw in the turbulence of nineteenth-century Romantic art a disregard for the historical distinction already made between the beautiful and the grotesque; and for that *ahistorical* affront to spirit's course, he might say, there is no justification—none, that is, unless one sees the continuing regard, the antiquarian nostalgia, for beauty in Hegel's own time as an imposed barrier to the telic possibilities of a new society. This is the modernist view that adopts Hegel's notion of progress while denying both his taste and his politics. This view considers the continuing preoccupation with the beauties of past art in fin de siècle society not as a philosophical quest but, rather, as prudential and self-serving; and it regards this stance as both aesthetically and politically decadent. The shift in the subject of appreciation becomes a critique of that decadence, and this extends the historical capacity of art as an epistemic symbol into modern times.

A new set of conditions for appreciation are here identified, of which beauty is not one.

Modernism has it that Hegel was premature in reporting the demise of art but that, in general, he is right about its progress. Hegel's legacy to modernism is the thesis that all aesthetic values can be brought into question, emended, or discarded—all, that is, except progress. As long as art and progress are linked, however, death continues to threaten. The next crisis occurs when the conditions of appreciation in modernism are challenged. This crisis generates a new theory about art in which it, art, goes on but does not progress—and need not die; the theory is known to us as "postmodernism."

III

MODERNISM AND POSTMODERNISM

SEVEN

Form, Intention Criticism

1. RECAPITULATION

AT THIS point, my narrative of thematic development reaches the period of modernism. The origins of this period can be traced back into the nineteenth-century, but its conclusion, when and whether it has ended, and why, is not at all clear. The term itself must take some blame for this. "Modernism" is both a name and a value judgment; to end the period is also to leave behind the beliefs that make "being modern" a good thing. In the last chapters of this book, I describe modernism as a particular transformation of the themes that are my general subject, and I trace the passage of this period into the one we presently call "postmodernism," through a further transformation—an inversion—of modernist beliefs. I conclude with a thematic characterization of postmodernism. However, before my discussion of these issues begins, a brief review is in order.

In the preceeding chapters, I locate the aesthetic theories of Kant, Schopenhauer, and Hegel in the contributions they make to the overall philosophical systems. I then trace these theories through certain themes that, in later history, gain a degree of independence. In their systematic roles these theories, despite their individual differences, have in common an epistemic function: They present their aesthetic subjects as providers of philosophically important knowledge. When the epistemic claims of these theories are eventually discarded, as by and large they have been in modern philosophy, the value placed on the aesthetic is redirected. Aesthetic value becomes internal to the interpretation of art, and the direction of its influence is reversed: It moves outward from these interpretations onto whatever else may be identified as also a concern of art. This redirection parallels the general abandonment in philosophy, during the early twentieth century, of the claim to systematic comprehensiveness: the claim that, say, a certain ontological stance entails a particular ethical view, or that aesthetic judgment corroborates the form of empirical knowledge. Of course, even in their original settings, the strength of "entails," "corroborates," and other such terms, depends on the limitations each system sets upon itself; Kant's limits, for example, are greater in this regard than Hegel's. But when these inferential connections are no longer offered at all, then such umbrella terms as "systematic" and "comprehensive," when applied to different areas of philosophy, increasingly become symptoms of piety; and these areas are then freed to make their own, often nonphilosophical, alliances. Thus, we see the current movement of epistemology toward cognitive science, ethics toward law, and aesthetics toward—perhaps even past—the boundaries between art and nonart.

My recasting of the originary aesthetic theories into the more insular themes of "taste," "expression," and "progress" examples an early version of this disengagement from systematic concerns. But at this juncture, the aesthetic still retains much of what philosophy (still) regards as its own domain: the noumenal suggestiveness of natural beauty as in Kant, the epistemic probing of irrationality as in Schopenhauer, or the rationalization of history as with Hegel. It is not until later that the notion of aesthetic instrumentality for concerns such as these is itself questioned, and the autonomy of art—the freedom to choose or reject alliances according to the internal imperatives of style—itself becomes an aesthetic value.

My objective in the present chapter is to trace the development of these strands of theory into the ideologies of modernism. In that period, as a consequence of disengagement from earlier theoretical concerns, the aesthetic and the artistic are at their most intimate, the former serving as the source of ideology, of interpretative justifications, for the latter. However, despite the apparent theoretical autonomy that this alliance provides the practice of art, I propose to show that the various strategies that modernist interpretations adopt become clearer, more interesting, perhaps even more credible, when they are traced back to their earlier sources. At the least, through such a hermeneutics, some philosophical reasons for art's new claim to autonomy can be identified and, subsequently, questioned.

In Chapters Eight and Nine I pursue these themes in the other direction. My argument there is that the particular conjunctions of art and theory in modernism did not provide an ongoing standard for the future, and that it is precisely their sundering, and the consequent theoretical, and social, indifference to artistic autonomy, that best characterizes our postmodernist present.

2. FROM TASTE TO FORM

I continue my discussion of these developing strands of theory by recasting the themes "taste," "expression," and "progress" into their modernist successors "form," "intention," and "criticism." I mark the redirection of aesthetic theory, in each case, by this change of name, and I begin with the transition from "taste" to "form."

The Kantian object of taste is an object shorn of all practical trappings: Utility, cost, circumstances of location and ownership, even existence, are discounted for appreciation. Although Kant imposes this singular status onto the object by his requirements for the *exercise* of taste, in later theory these requirements become the characteristics for which the thing, in its status as "artwork," is *itself* valued. They become the normative criteria of the theory of interpretation we know as "formalism." Here, the modern aporia over form and content emerges. The distinction between form and content, between, say, the "how" and "what" of depictions or descriptions, is an unwelcome one for formalist aesthetics, in that this distinction purports to divide what is, or should be considered, a unity. Also unwelcome is that the apparent symmetry of the division is not really between equals: the one side, form, being the necessary locus of aesthetic value; the other, content, merely a catchall for historically contingent uses of art.

Nevertheless, the denial of this distinction is problematic for formalist assessments of older art because traditional works seem to sustain the distinction more easily than do modern ones, and yet they cannot plausibly be devalued on this account. In the visual arts, one way to get past the intrusions of antiquated or intrusive subject matter is to deny that it is important and to direct aesthetic value to, for example, the mastery with which shape and color and space are harmonized. Of course, taking this tack risks relegating iconographic studies to an extra-aesthetic limbo; but, more importantly, it evokes a curious kind of distinction between modern and traditional art. The latter, the formalist could say, is a "two-tiered" art, in that its formal accomplishments are presented in the guise of publicly warranted fictions. Such an art is "preautonomous" because its general social acceptance, even existence, depends on its mimetic servitude, but its underlying aesthetic accomplishments persist, even flourish, in the rarified context of connoisseurship. This double tiering identifies, and requires, a society that is itself stratified, one in which art functions at once as a didactic social instrument, imaging the world in permissible ways, and as an aesthetically edifying instrument for cultivated sensibilities. In this context, annunciations, apotheoses, and great victories confirm belief and allegiance; they also provide a distinct, aesthetic pleasure. For the moderns who disdain, at least those, beliefs and allegiances, that pleasure remains for the acute formal discrimination. This "supervenience" of interpretations preserves aesthetic value for traditional art.

But formalism is also recognized as a specifically Modernist ideology and, for that context, it does not countenance an art that is functionally divided. Its program demands that the formal virtues masked by traditional contents achieve autonomy by *becoming* the content of modern art. Here, formalism's secondary debt to Hegel is apparent. When one identifies artistic autonomy with the identity of form and content, it is tantamount to setting aside all of art's external obligations, even those of describing the world. This, in turn, signals, not yet the end of art, but the end of art as an academic profession. For art to reach this position of autonomy, it must progress beyond its earlier historical, aesthetic and social, constraints. Under this view, the formalist aesthetic is not only a Kantian description of what (timelessly) constitutes aesthetic value; it is a Hegelian historical achievement: It is the ideological support for an art whose concern (finally) is with nothing but the projection of its own formal value.

In various ways, the identification of form as an aesthetic value can be traced back through the history of art, but my concern here is with its influence on the ideologies of art making through the nineteenth century into modernism. Although this influence can be found in all the arts, its adequate documentation would require a separate study, so I limit my remarks to the visual arts.

The exemplifying sequence of form in modernism moves from a direct concern with nature toward abstraction and nonobjectivity. I begin this tracing with Cézanne, whose preoccupation with landscape I take to mirror the philosophical role Kant assigns the appreciation of natural beauty. While Cézanne followed the "direct observation" dictum of the Impressionists, he criticized them for being satisfied with "surface" and "ephemerals." His own program aimed at transforming sensory experience into the geometric structures that he *knew* underlay the immediate givens of natural appearances.[1] An analogy can be made between this program and the relationship Kant establishes between sense data and the categories of the understanding, for in both cases, sensory imput is viewed as inchoate unless organized, given form, by an active cognition. Pertinent examples of Cézanne's works here would be the Bibemus Quarry paintings, and the late watercolors, circa 1880–1902.

This stylistic tracing of form can be continued into the early cubism of Picasso and Braque, with its evident emulations of Cézanne, and then into monuments of analytic cubism such as Picasso's *Portrait of Kahnweiler* of 1910 and Braque's *Man with Guitar* of 1911, works where mimetic evocations and structural self-reference come together in an exquisitely precarious balance.[2] It may be that the content, as well as the value, of these works is located precisely in this balance, rather than in their historical premonitions. Here, one can recollect the balance, between the physical and spiritual god, that Hegel so admired in classical art.

The many abstract and nonobjective styles that proliferated in pre–World War II Europe shifted this balance away from mimetic elements and toward a preoccupation with "pure" form. Cubism, with its pervasive influence, was often identified as an antecedent of this shift; Mondrian, for example, considered his abstract works (after about 1915) as "logical developments" of cubism. The early works of Kandinsky, on the other hand, had their sources in Fauvism and Expressionism.[3] Nevertheless, whatever their specific lineage, all these works shared the ideological imprimatur of fulfilling a central modernist goal—that of establishing a self-referential art. Viewing modernism in this light, however, again raises the issue referred to above, namely, the relationship between the two values that uneasily inhabit the theme of formalism: the correlation of form with artistic autonomy, and the identification of form with the development of historical style. This needs a further look.

In its philosophical role, autonomy is a Kantian propaedeutic for morality, and within his aesthetic, art sustains the role of morality's symbol. In this sense, a self-referential art can be seen as particularly compatible with "disinterestedness" in appreciation, which, in turn, is compatible with the purely rational will that is a condition of moral judgment—pure form provides few venial distractions. However, while this glossing of autonomies and their high purposes does act as a philosophical justification for art, it also weakens art's claim to its *own* autonomy: Being morality's symbol is not self-reference. The question then arises whether the conflation of the two values of aesthetic formalism, autonomy *as* self-reference, is tenable. One can argue against this by showing that, historically, art has done quite well with nonaesthetic obligations, indeed, that its value, whether philosophical or aesthetic, has often been enhanced through such obligations. Under this reading, then, it would seem either that art does not require autonomy to function as art or, at the least, that autonomy is not self-reference. To avoid this theoretical difficulty, formalism can be interpreted another way: as a designation of a particular achievement of style. Autonomy and self-reference can then be retained by identifying them with the characteristics of, say, abstract and nonobjective art. But this interpretation has its own difficulties, for under it, formalism includes the thesis of a historically *increasing* artistic autonomy (a Hegelian gambit) and must be normatively skewed toward modern art.

There is another interpretation, however, that rescues formalism from being circumscribed as the ideology of a particular style. Here, the move is to disengage autonomy from self-reference. Under this interpretation, formalism can be taken as claiming, not that an art of pure form is an achievable ideal, but that what is both important and constant in art is its formal structure. This separates formalism from Hegel's teleology and returns it to its Kantian origins where it functions as a (preferred) mode of perception. Affirming the aesthetic primacy of form also expands the applicability, given some finessing, of the theory to past, present, and even future art. With art thus normatively rather than stylistically united, the assertion that formal value does not depend on but, rather, *transcends* historical change becomes more coherent. Given this reading, however, what the theory must do is make explicit its often unvoiced, but central, assumption: It must show that there is a good way to distinguish form that has aesthetic value from form that does not. This explication is necessary because form, stripped of all stylistic commitment, is ubiquitous and universally applicable—everything has form. Therefore, use of the term as a normative distinction requires us to specify the *kind* of form we mean.

A well-known attempt to cope with this problem is found in the "significant form" theory of Clive Bell.[4] I present it here as a clear early account of formalist aesthetics. Although Bell's famous essay asks the question, What is art? he does not venture into the ontological issues that so attract later theory. Bell's question is normative, for its actual subject is, What is aesthetically good in art? Accordingly, his concern is to specify what it is about artworks that makes some more valuable than others, and his answer is that, in some, the form is more "significant" than in others. Through this answer he equates aesthetic value with a work's formal qualities—thus minimizing representational and intentional factors in aesthetic judgment. The apparent circularity of Bell's thesis has often been noted: that to the question how we know significant form when we see it (his concern was primarily with the visual arts), he answers—when we are stirred by an "aesthetic emotion"; and to the question when we are so stirred, he answers—when in the presence of significant form. Actually, I call this circularity "apparent" because it can be resolved by appeal to a thesis that Bell did not articulate but, like others of his generation, must have taken for granted: the Humean criterion of "competent judges."[5] I introduce it here because I feel that this criterion, its strengths and vulnerabilities, is essential to the credibility of formalist aesthetics. Hume's argument is that our anticipations of continued regularity in nature, which we ascribe to "laws," are nothing but our habituations to experiences of prior regularities. In thus correlating law with habit, Hume shows an epistemic skepticism that anticipates and influences Kant's categorial organization of thought.[6] But despite Hume's skepticism, he does not deny the legitimacy of *making* judgments about connections between events; for him, our experiences of regularity provide us with the only certainty we need, or can have.

In the context of aesthetic judgment, the attribution of

"significance" to form is much like applying "necessity" to events. Both gain the objectivity, hence, justification, for the judgment from the regularities of the past. "Habit" assumes its aesthetic guise in "competent judges": The individual defers judgment to those who, by virtue of experience, background, and character, can best adjudicate on a given issue. This is the role Bell assigns to criticism, a role authenticated by appeal to "all sensitive people" and "the best opinion."[7] When asked, therefore, how we know that a form is significant and, hence, that the emotion it stirs in us is truly aesthetic, Bell could reply: if we are competent to judge. This answer allies Bell's thesis with the Kantian affinity between the aesthetic and moral in appreciation. It also allies Bell with a "gradualist" model of social and aesthetic progress, the model that presumes a continuity between earlier and later forms, such that a body of experts and expertise can be called upon to produce the criteria through which we, some of us, can learn to make the proper judgments. But is this argument entirely sound?

If there is a tension to be found in Bell's thesis, it is not in the interdependency of "significant form" and "aesthetic emotion," it is in deciding who, in social fact, are the competent judges. Some perspective is needed here. While a need for the adjudicating function of a body of experts survived the historical turn to modernism, it was marked by the substitution of one body for another: ideologues of the avant-garde for apologists of the academy. Paradoxically, Bell himself presents a Nietzschean challenge to the gradualist belief that the tradition of art has been and continues to be nurtured by the "best opinion." Here, the question of competence becomes a social as well as aesthetic demarcator. When faced with the general resistance to the demands "significant form" imposes on appreciation, Bell grandiloquently contrasts "the superb peaks of aesthetic exaltation" with "the snug foothills of warm humanity." The contrast comes to this: At the historical juncture when the central aesthetic value, form, becomes the primary concern of art and can be directly experienced in appreciation, the audience divides along the, now familiar, lines of uncomprehending bourgeois and exhortatory radicals. Here is Bell's parting admonition: "And let no one imagine, because he has made merry in the warm tilth and quaint nooks of romance, that he can even guess at the austere and thrilling raptures of those who have climbed the cold white peaks of art."[8] This admonition signals the modernist transformation of Hume's competent judge from adjudicator of taste to critic of the social order. "Warm humanity" is now the enemy of art, and the critic an inhabitant of Zarathustra's mountaintop.[9]

In Chapter Eight, I describe a fundamental challenge to the critical absolutism of the formalist aesthetic, especially to the thesis that its authority is maintained through the discriminating judgments of those who have the capacity to so judge. The challenge is to the very notion of "aesthetic capacity," to the centers of critical authority, the institutions that are its didactic sources, and, by extension, to the notion of a historical constancy of succession between such centers. I take this challenge to be one signal of the end of modernism.

3. FROM EXPRESSION TO INTENTION

The second thematic transition I examine moves from art as "expression" to art as "intention." I link these terms together in order to identify an aesthetic that places primary value on creative process and thus presents appreciation with the task of retrieving that process. My concern here is not with the recent debates over the problem of "intentionality"—whether the retrieval of artistic intentions is either impossible or necessary in the interpretation of artworks.[10] I do not take this issue, put this way, to be a decidable one, for it seems to be more a debate over stylistic preference and the location of aesthetic value than over the limits of theory: As not all artworks direct attention to their origins and to the attributes of their makers, then, if we are interested in such things, we pay attention to the ones that do; and aesthetic theories that authenticate such factors for interpretation invariably select certain artworks rather than others as their exemplars.

The modern label "Expressionism" identifies works that are generally understood as both exhibiting and referring to the conditions of their origins.[11] These conditions are interpreted as going beyond the "making" into the "intent" of the maker; and a confluence, however determined, between these two, intent and making, is one mark of aesthetic value. All intentions are not equal, however, in that their holders, artists, also profess values of a nonaesthetic sort—moral, political, et cetera—which, under this theory, bear directly on the value of their aesthetic intentions and, transitively, on the value of the works. Artistic expression, then, is not only a simple magnitude or "capacity," it is also a compatibility between the intentional origins of that expression and issues of deep general concern. Artistic intentions must be worth retrieving; they are not all equally valuable.

In Schopenhauer, the primary sense of expression is metaphysical: Will "expresses itself" through the world it constantly creates and destroys. The dynamics of the action are matched only by its pointlessness. *Artistic* expression, here, is actually the antagonist of this process, for the images of art do not celebrate the will but, rather, seek to go beyond it, to a Parmenidean world of stasis and essence. In a similar sense, Schopenhauer does not model creative activity on the processes of the will. His artist does not, for example, appropriate the dramatics of nature's acts of building and tearing down. Artistic creativity retains its cognitive purpose: The aim is to know the world rather than to embody it in action. However, there is also the historical premonition of Romanticism here. Schopenhauer's artist no longer enjoys the Enlightenment unity of purpose and subject. The world that art reveals in the nineteenth century has become duplicitous, and the cost to the artist of these revelations is couched in the Expressionist imagery of a divided self.

These divisions can be traced back to Kant: to the nature that he positions between beauty and sublimity, where appreciation is sometimes assaulted by its subject, and thus betrayed. The growing indifference to beauty after Kant relocates this division wholly within sublimity, and it is here that expression becomes identified with artistic intention. Sublimity encompasses both inchoate boundlessness and oppressive immediacy: the infinite heavens and the sudden storm. The experience of sublimity, accordingly, fluctuates between exaltation and fear. The fear is engendered by the threat that oppressive nature poses to the rational self—the threat of death for no good reason. The exaltation marks the overcoming of this threat through a "becoming as one" with nature: Sublimity's content is achieved through a reciprocating action, not through thought's disinterested scrutiny. The Romantic embrace of nature's histrionics identifies creativity with the natural sublime and, in doing so (a move that Schopenhauer might have thought trivial), replaces the will with the artistic psyche. The artist now becomes the repository of nature's "secrets," and ontological truth is reached through a psychological tracing of creative process to its source in artistic intention. Nature, here, loses the negativity that Schopenhauer gives it and comes to be seen as a symbol of freedom, one that is able to reconcile the opposition between purity and extravagance. Nature's power is neither evil nor crude. The artist, in emulating, in becoming "as," nature, becomes, in effect, the Romantic symbol of virtue, a virtue of instinct and action rather than of deliberation. This is the Dionysian artist of Nietzsche and Wagner.[12]

But the perversity of Schopenhauer's will does not entirely disappear in Romanticism; it is relocated in the workings of conventional—later, bourgeois—society. When the notion of "will" is traced from its metaphysical origins to its later use as a metaphor for societal ambitions and aggressions, the Romantic emphasis on artistic expression can then be interpreted as a confrontation with the hidden, read as "hypocritical," motives behind these conventionalized drives. This confrontation sets up another series of oppositions, now between individual values and group mores and, more generally, between art and society. Here, artistic activity remains revelatory, but its content shifts from noumenal to psychological probity. Artists express themselves by revealing themselves, by showing others how the world is to a psyche whose layerings have open pathways between them, where motives, needs, and acts are transparent to one another. The intent of the artist, under this theory, is achieved through a "deep diving," but its bottom is not "will" but "id," not an image of essences but of the subconscious. The alternative to social duplicity is the truth inherent in the psychic origins of personality, a truth distorted by the social pressures and rewards of conformity. There is no deceit in the id, anymore than there is in the natural sublime; and those most open to its impulses—savages, hermits, artists, the insane—are those closest to a truth that, depending on one's perspective, can remake the world or, at least, give authenticity to the self.

Schopenhauer's perils of creativity remain in force:

neurosis, alienation, the expressive urge as self-destructive. But increasingly, as modernism takes hold, artists' efforts are heralded as symbols of a psychological courage that, if we dared, could be a model for us all. The capacity for originality is now equated with such daring. The truth that Schopenhauer finds in the images of art becomes the modernist value of artistic freedom. The antagonism here is between "expression" and "repression": As the images of art are a denial of the repressions of the will, so the artistic act is a denial of psychological repression, which, in turn, comes to be seen as the rejection of a repressive social order. The artist's expressive life is the modernist symbol of emancipation.

"Seeking the artist in the work" identifies the functional question of retrieval—seeking the origins of expression. This is a broader question than is usually associated with intentionality, for it encompasses unconscious as well as conscious processes; but it has its well-known difficulties. For one, how are such processes to be ascertained? It is a commonplace that explanations are of little value here, not only because of obtuseness or duplicity, but because the origins and motives of creative activity remain mysterious, to the artist as well as to others. Even as Schopenhauer's will is obscured by social conventions, so the basis for individual creativity is hidden under the repetitions of style. It might be said that the Expressionist mystique is a secretive one and abhors explanation; and an artist's attempt to articulate the origins of the creative impulse is often taken as a sign of shallowness—the cover-up for a loss of nerve before the abyss of primary process. For Schopenhauer, contemplation is hindered by the narrative of achievement; the ascetic's experience resists its documentation—for then the experience would become one of ambition and, thus, a capitulation to the will. In a similar sense, artists need neither explicate nor even understand the sources of their work; they must, however, be able to reach these sources. And artworks, on their part, must show the traces of this effort so that its path can be followed in appreciation.

But this does not resolve the difficulty: How do artworks document artistic intentions? The answer calls for some reference to artworks. Schopenhauer's view on the particular arts is that music, because it structurally resembles the dynamics of emotional life, functions as a direct analogue of the will as process. For my examples in the visual arts, it would be tempting to choose artists whose works are marked by strong pictorial rhythm and an emphasis on process: Van Gogh and Soutine are evident candidates and, certainly, the Expressionist works of Kandinsky. I take another approach, however, that emphasizes a different aspect of Schopenhauer's aesthetic, his thesis of a reality outside the will and of the visual arts as a still mirror of the Platonic Forms. I place this thesis into the context of subconscious imagery, the context of surrealist art. I do this because the sources of surrealist imagery: dreams, fantasies, hallucinations, have also been described as pathways to a reality that is more basic than the one of "ordinary" consciousness. This is the Apollonian legacy of Nietzsche and Freud.[13]

The development of surrealism, as contrasted with the abstract movements in modern art, did not involve a rejection of mimetic imagery; rather, it identified a new region for picturing—the world of the subconscious—and sought for procedures of retrieval and portrayal that would be adequate to that region. The paintings of Odilon Redon can be cited as early examples. Such works as *Chariot of Apollo* of 1910 have sources in both fantasy and myth, thereby authenticating the individual images of the former by their presence in the collective imagery of the latter. This mutuality in source identifies a central ideology of Surrealist art: that its value does not rest merely on the facilitation of individual access to a repressed psyche. If this were all, the value would remain merely personal and therapeutic. Rather, the claim is that the subconscious, in its important sense, is collective, and that private images are also manifestations of the "universal archetypes" of myth, ritual, and religion.[14] Interpretations of these archetypes through art produce an explanatory power that rivals science, as these are interpretations of forces that underlie the ones identified by empirical procedures. Schopenhauer's twin concepts of the will as existentially veiled by its representations and the ontological primacy of will over representation can thus be seen as central to surrealism.

Access to the subconscious in the context of psychoanalysis involves the now familiar techniques of dream analysis, free association, and projection. Pictorial access to this realm, during the early stages of surrealism, called for new imaging procedures: the bypassing of conscious control through techniques of chance and automatism, and the clash of contexts provoked by collage and frottage. The issue of subjective access also rekindled interest in the fantastic art of the past—Bosch, Breugel, Goya. With this latter thrust, surrealism risked ignoring the modernist opprobrium on traditional art by adapting certain "old master" techniques to the representation of surrealist imagery. In the paintings of Max Ernst one finds a virtual catalogue of such ideas and methods: The work *Vision Provoked by the Words "Immovable Father"* of 1927 probes the repressed psyche by focusing ambiguous imagery through an evocative title, thereby appropriating literature as a proper part of painting. In the frottage *Naturelle* of 1925, free associations are built upon rubbings taken from an old wall, thereby projecting meanings into the nominally meaningless. And in *The Temptations of St. Anthony* of 1945, a full demonology of the subconscious is presented through techniques adapted from Flemish art. Here, in a look back to Schopenhauer, both style and psychic processes are placed outside the control of history or teleology.

Such surrealist works demonstrate one of the basic divisions through which I characterize modernism. If the theme of form commits art to the values of purity and abstraction, intention permits it to revel in the discontinuous and the excessive. In the first context, the distortions of pictorial space and canons of proportion in early modernism are interpreted as but passing steps toward the elimination of all mimetic cues; this is the theme of form in the guise of "abstraction." In the context of surrealist art, however, such distortions mirror the logic of a world arrived at through the imagination, one structured according to the canons of dream and fantasy. In this sense, they also function mimetically, for they provide us with a "true likeness" of that world. The distortions of surrealist art thus come to be canonical in their own system and, as such, cannot be called distortions. Also, although some may go deeper than others, none go further; thus, none are supervened by historical process.

Yet, in the development of modernism, a problem arises in this thematic category that is analogous to the problem of ubiquity for the theme of form. In the postwar period, the growing popularity of depth psychology and the therapeutic value of expression push the concern with artistic creativity in the direction of style rather than source. Artists' anxieties and uncertainties, mistakes and false starts, translate into the increasingly familiar methodologies of the new American art. We follow, and find, the artist in the gesticulations, cacaphonies, and exclamations in the works and, given the increasing numbers of both artists and works, we dispense with the further search for a unique psyche: The once-elusive intentions now have a common image and a method for their portrayal. In the visual arts, the style of Abstract Expressionism, which came into dominance during the 1950s and 1960s, brings together formalist, expressionist, and surrealist values into a common aesthetic: Syntax, the "form of feeling," becomes more significant than reference; and syntax, as befitting an academic discipline, can be learned. Here, abstraction keeps its distance from the self-reference of form, preferring, instead, the persona of the stone wall, whose rubbings evoke whatever imagination can muster itself to see.[15] This turn of history creates the most available and democratic of artistic styles—but it is at some remove from Schopenhauer's artist or the content of his quest.

This transformation in value, from the uniqueness of intentions to their commonality, has important social ramifications. In late modernism, the aesthetics of expression signal the new democratization of art. The search for origins comes to reveal, not a unique, self-immolating psyche, but "everyman," soon to become "everyperson." Evidently, a society that has survived a severe testing of communal values through a war with irrational ideologies will want its art to express a kindred rather than alien spirit. In this move away from elitism and marginality, evidence of individual artistic effort takes on the trappings of a common language, and the familiarity of its syntax signals that effort's success. Intention's recursive path now points to the socially integrated psyche.

This consequence also points to the ideal of a socially integrated art, providing as well a (welcome) end to the Romantic "conflict between art and life." The artistic autonomy gained at the price of social alienation is now superseded by images of a communal style; and the evidence for expressiveness comes to be identified with the earmarks of that style. The concept of expression no longer supports Schopenhauer's exceptional linkage between alienation, insight, and value; like its counterpart "form," it has become ubiquitous in its realm: Just as everything has form, we all express ourselves—all the time.

This turn of theory points to a conclusion that is conceptually intriguing but eventually becomes untenable for modernist aesthetics, namely, that all activities are expressive and, hence, that everyone is an artist. As with the aesthetics of formalism, if the theory is not to disintegrate, *some* distinctions are needed, although they may no longer require Schopenhauer's linkage between alienation and metaphysical truth. Still, creativity and truth remain a potent combination for theory, and the solution to the above dilemma may be to retain these and discard alienation. This solution is also suggested by the success of a different linkage: Good taste, even when removed from Kant's systematic role, remains an exemplification of the manners and mores of a privileged class. Creativity, however, unlike taste, does not easily sustain public morality: Even when it is redirected from will to id, artistic expression reveals a world that, however true, *is* antithetic to the social weal—id impulses are no guide for communal behavior. The problem, then, becomes one of establishing a linkage between expression and morality, and the solution, again, may be to discard alienation.

One well-known version of this solution is found in the aesthetic writings of Leo Tolstoi, writings that, in part, retain their influence because the author's artistic achievements provide a particularly intimate source for his theoretical inquiry.[16] Taking the brotherhood of man to be of more consequence than aesthetic entities (his own included), Tolstoi treats the artwork as a mere conduit through which the "infection" of a populist Christianity can be transmitted from the artist to the social order. The sincerity and emotional depth of the artist are conjoined with the innocence and receptivity of the audience. They come together in a "common," in the sense both of "mutual" and "classless," understanding. Put this way, his thesis provides one of the strong arguments for intentionality in interpretation, in that the artist is seen as the source of aesthetic value, the work being merely a means of transmission, and the audience a generalized beneficiary. But I suggest that Tolstoi's real source is elsewhere, for he takes artistic intentions as valuable only if they are the right kind. Tolstoi argues against a certain construal of the artist-audience relationship, that of the "professional" serving the "societal elite." His socialist theories are at issue here: Art that caters to decadence, notwithstanding any formal or expressive virtues it might have, must itself be decadent, and so must the artist who provides it. The artist qua professional is in thrall. His artistic intentions, the purported base of his expressiveness, do not count for appreciation because no one really wants to know. What does count for professionalism is expertise and manner. Content is worked out in negotiations, and commissions define and circumscribe expression. Within this agreement, formal virtues are free to develop.

Given his dislike of his own socially stratified culture, and having himself as an exemplar, one first expects that Tolstoi would find his social aims compatible with the notion of "expressive freedom." This notion, when coupled with Tolstoi's social programs, could also be compatible with a new equivalence between artist and audience, one calling for a transaction between them, a theoretical and normative pact, that would relegate the artwork to the tertiary role of doing what it must to keep matters clear. If the artist is seen here as the originary source of the "infection," the values to be transmitted, it could follow that "artist," for this theory, is the source of aesthetic value. But this conclusion would be a mistake. Tolstoi, as Plato, has a deep suspicion of private sentiments: For both, the value is in *what* is expressed and not in the exercise. Tolstoi makes no inference from the quality of expression to its content, although he does make the reverse inference. There is no romantic cult of the individual here. Rather, the exercise of artistic freedom is understood in the theological sense of conformity with revealed truth: One is not free when one errs, only capricious. Granted, Tolstoi's artist can be viewed as a social (if not artistic) advance over the status of "professional," in that autobiography, belief, and sincerity do count for him. But these count only as testimonials to the wanted ideal, not as its determinants. It is true that artist and audience are joined in a social contract effected by the transparency of the artwork and agreement about the moral will. But this contract requires a surveillance across the bridge of the work, meant to insure both rightness of artistic sensibility and of its issue. Tolstoi had a mystical faith in the "intrinsic goodness" of the peasantry, seeing it as both reason and testimonial to Christ's coming. As such, it is the determinant of the ideal that needs articulating by art. Artistic success depends on whether it shares in that goodness, whether the artist is in some sense, as Tolstoi tried to be, also a peasant. The virtues of artistic genius are retained here, but their psychic origins are located in the requirements of a social class and are thus specified.

This specification turns Tolstoi's aesthetic of intentionality into an instrumentalist theory. Indeed, it may well be that all such aesthetics are, more or less examined, versions of instrumentalism. In the originary theories here under discussion, the artistic process is ontologically instrumental—for its content is an exposition of nature, will, spirit. A century later, having survived the intervening perils of psychic and social alienation, artistic expression comes to symbolize a different desideratum: the fusion of individual autonomy and communal values. The problem in late modernism is whether this *aesthetic* instrumentality, and its products, can any longer be distinguished from other activities that also presume to do the same thing.

4. FROM PROGRESS TO CRITICISM

My third thematic transition is the move from "progress" to "criticism." Of the three, this historical event is most closely linked with modernism, for it signals the discord between artistic innovation and art's social role that is characterized by the term "avant-garde."[17] The military origins of this term, a scouting and attack party deployed ahead of the main force, transfers easily into the aesthetic meaning where art's role is seen as that of a gadfly promoting the values of the future. Art and society are here disjoined: The conflict between them occurs when the present is being hurried into the past because it is at the point where the future can be symbolized. This recognition of, and infatuation with, the future undermines the present because it undermines the durability and satisfactions of achievement. Works of art come to be prized more for their suggestiveness of further transformation than for what they have arrived at. Appreciation is thus separated from enjoyment and directed toward prediction. But these anticipations of the future hold no promise of respite, of a lull where the "future-present" can be savored through a reconnection with its past. Instead, the avant-garde construal of progress constitutes a generational criticism of the present for having, or, at least, acknowledging, a past, a criticism prompted by the fear that such acknowledgment will vitiate momentum toward the future. For those who wish to live as comfortably as possible within their allotted time—a condition historically identified with the bourgeoisie—such criticism is largely unwelcome. So, the aesthetic theme of progress is transformed into criticism when it is rejected, when its symbols are identified with the values and demands of radical political ideology.

It is difficult to choose the artist that best exemplifies this theme, for there are so many good candidates. Indeed, the very notion of modernism seems to require the thesis that art progresses, and there are few artworks that at all fit this label that do not stake their value on their supersedence of some valuable past art. So I must base my choice on a fine-tuning of the theme of progress, namely, on the degree of discontinuity between past and present that a work's self-presentation evokes, for a high degree signifies the "critical" turn in my narrative of transformation.

Kasimir Malevich, perhaps more than other artists of the avant-garde, defined the content of his works through a fusion of form and ideology. These works, the Suprematist paintings, circa 1910–25, are of an iconic simplicity and offer little gratification in matters of painterly virtues. In fact, the historical challenge of these works is located precisely in the claim that they are art of great consequence *because* they have minimized such virtues. These works project a sense of finality, of having brought artistic sensibility to the edge of "pure idea," to the point of dematerialization beyond which a painting can no longer remain a sensual object. Through this achievement, they become both a rebuttal and extension of Hegel's categorical scheme. Yet, these works continue to be paintings by virtue of the exquisite balance Malevich maintains between matter and spirit, art and idea. In the *White on White* of 1918, a just off-white square is tilted diagonally on a differently off-white larger square. Here, contrast is minimized but the dynamics of asymmetry maintained. In *Black Square* of 1915, a black square is placed symmetrically on a larger white square. Here, value contrast is emphasized and placement is dynamically neutral. Having reached this point, Malevich did not, to my knowledge, take the next—perhaps logical, but no longer pictorial—step. He did not, for example, place a white square symmetrically on another white square; for that would not have been a fulfillment but an attack on all that had gone before.

For Malevich, these paintings did not signify the "end of art." Reaching this edge was not a move toward nihilism but rather a welcome transformation in both art and society; the end was also a beginning. At the time these paintings were created, the modernist alliance between the themes of form and progress supported the view that representational concerns were a thing of the past. The only question that remained pressing was whether the transformation of mimetic concerns into purely formal ones would be on the model of historical gradualism, as in Cubism or Fauvism, or whether the demise should be abrupt and dramatic, a gesture of will, as heralded by the abstract turn of Malevich and other artists allied with Suprematism and Constructivism.[18] But this question, about the degree of discontinuity a given process can tolerate, is much the same one that was then being asked about the process of social transformation. These aesthetically radical works began their development in the disintegrating Russian society of the First World War, and they continued as part of the radicalized Soviet society after the revolution, 1914–24. In the latter part of this brief period, avant-garde art became an accepted style in the Soviet Union: Its emancipation from the older aesthetic forms gave it credibility as a symbol of the new social order, and its easy integration with architecture, planning, public art, made it a proper part of the new collective enterprise. All this was brought to an end by Stalin's purge of Trotsky; and the brief moment when progress was thought not to entail criticism was over.[19] The destruction of these ideals, and the consequent history of radical movements in Europe, needs no retelling here.

The relationship between the theme of "criticism" and the themes already discussed, "form" and "intention," is complex. As all three reject the academic constraints and obligations of traditional art forms, this shared belief in the new art identifies them all as modernist values. The transition from their earlier identities can also be explained through their interplay. The theme of "progress" becomes the ideological catalyst for the move into modernism: "Taste" makes the transition to "form" when its objects are purified—and that is a historical achievement, progress in the evolution of style. "Expression," in like manner, is also subject to progress—when "intention" is freed from marginality and becomes an exemplary source of communal value.

However, the relationship between the three themes becomes antagonistic when progress-turned-criticism attempts to maintain its ascendency through the claim that sustaining progress is the central value of modernism and that the other themes can impede this effort. The theme of criticism is then (critically) leveled at the "accommodative" tendencies of formalism: that in the move to secure autonomy for the tradition of art, form allies itself with any institutional power that offers autonomy and, thus, art's role as a cultural gadfly is undermined. Interpreted this way, the formalist ideal of autonomy has the unwelcome consequence of trivializing and thus contributing to the eventual irrelevance of art.

The theme of intentionality is also subject to criticism, and it is charged with confusing a central aesthetic value with its peripheral application. Expression, in the context of progress, is one of art's transformative functions and, thereby, furthers its symbolic potency for social change. When the search for the sources of expression degenerates into the therapeutic function of reconciling individual differences and social norms, art's transformative powers are weakened. Here, the unwanted consequence is not art's irrelevance, but its eventual indiscernibility.

Through this sort of polemic, "criticism" proposes itself as the encompassing aesthetic value of modernism. It offers the other themes credibility by justifying their historical development, but it admonishes them for partiality and historical naïveté. Progress become criticism looks at art from the dual standpoint of the "engaged other;" and the dialectical restlessness of its Hegelian source precludes, so the argument goes, the ideological stasis of mere engagement or mere otherness: conformity or irrelevance.

In retrospect, however, it seems evident that of the three values at issue, "art as criticism" has itself been most vulnerable to attack. The crucial problem is the Hegelian inheritance of teleology: Progress is coherent only as "progress toward," and criticism is an attack on inhibitions to progress—both entail an end. This inheritance need not affect the other themes: For example, one can conceive of form as an eternal self-renewing value, within which "better" and "worse" are not historically cumulative but, rather, recognitions of normative peaks and valleys throughout the history of art. Intention, in like manner, can be considered a heuristic gambit that is available at those times when the factor of artistic creativity becomes useful for the aims of interpretation. In contrast, criticism presents itself as the militant arm of progress turned against historical relativism. However, as Hegel himself remarked, the security of this position is vulnerable to betrayal by the contingencies of history and, thus, to counterattack from all sides.

In their Hegelian origins, the themes of history and progress are already linked. For Hegel, however, while the history of art demonstrates that culture is progressing, the qualities of individual artworks give reassurance that such progress continues to head in the right direction. At the inception of modernism, few of its theoreticians would have denied that art is, in fact, must be, progressing, but there was little to reassure them about the direction. The social and political developments of the nineteenth and early twentieth centuries brought into question any theoretical rapprochement between either reason and nature, or reason and culture. As I point out above, one consequence of this was the emergence of the aesthetic values of formal autonomy and expressive freedom. When brought together through the synthesizing agency of the theme of progress, the resulting ideology becomes a powerful remonstration against society's refusal, through its attitudes toward its art, to respond to the self-evident need for cultural change. This, in effect, constitutes the thematic transformation from "progress" to "criticism."

The critical aspect of modern art, as exampled above by Malevich and his circle, is neither didactic nor exhortatory. This distinguishes it both from the older persuasions of traditional art and from the totalitarian "social realisms" that came soon after. Modernist criticism is leveled through artistic innovations and the extraordinary demands these innovations place on the audience. These demands, and the anticipated hostile reactions, foment a crisis in both appreciation and the greater society. One's attitudes toward modernist works become a signpost of one's political attitudes. Radical art implies radical politics, the term "avant-garde" applies to both, and in this context, both appreciation and social conscience require that one relinquish the confirmations of tradition for the dislocations of the new.

In early modernism, the ideological seriousness behind this demand overrode the fears that, in some measure, are voiced by all my philosophical protagonists—the difficulty of distinguishing between genuine newness and mere caprice.[20] Even for the most unlikely candidates, critically radicalized appreciation would search for signs of transformative value. Indeed, to produce an unlikely work was itself seen as a mark of authenticity in the artist's intentions. Whatever else it might be, the avant-garde work was not a test of the flexibility of artistic traditions; it did not demonstrate the extent to which styles could be adapted and reshaped within the stabilizing values of the past. Rather, in modernism's most heady days, such work was held to be an emancipation *from* tradition, in effect, a "tradition of the new" where all the old rules and suppressions no longer counted or could be critically enforced.[21]

The hope, of course, was that all this would eventually find its proper social context, that the artistic ideal, through its critical function, would help effect the social ideal. But this was not to be, or, at least, not in the ways then imagined. The aesthetic and social legacies of Hegel were sundered in the modernist period. The political ideologies in which "progress" was dogmatized by the requirements of power would brook no interference from the autonomies of either art or artist, and the condition of art's social servitude, once thought irrevocably past, was revived. It has often been noted that the so-called Hegelianisms of the right and left—the Nazi and Communist powers—were united in their distrust and suppression of avant-garde art, a suppression justified by the sophistry that a successful revolution requires an art that extols its achievements in the most socially "accessible" terms.

Some of the ideological aftermath of this period, tracing

these aesthetic themes past the traumas and dislocations of the Second World War, shows the conceptual weariness that historical perversion of belief is apt to inflict. Such weariness is also a Hegelian legacy, one consequence of his view of history, and it comes out of a disjunction between historical narrative and actual events, when events do not, and show no promise of, following the path that a rational teleology expects. Conceptual weariness is symptomatic of a universalized criticism redirected toward the self, when the beliefs underlying such criticism become historically untenable but remain existentially compelling and are not let go. I pursue this thematic turn through the work of Roland Barthes.

Barthes was one of the most influential exponents of the New Criticism that developed in postwar Europe. His work is difficult to characterize, since it combines the imaginative traits of belles lettres with pointed critical assaults on the new edifices of cultural and ideological power. These assaults are directed against modernist values that Barthes construes as having become dogmatic hindrances to the continuity of progress through their alliance with the notion of domination. In the following chapter, I explore the decline of modernism through the thesis that the aesthetic themes here at issue congeal into dogmas during the late stages of that period. I find some of these sentiments in Barthes, and in this sense, my analysis of his theories functions as a bridge to that discussion.

Although Barthes's criticisms have a Hegelian character, in that they aim at dismantling fixed categories through the exposure of contradictions and covert assumptions, Barthes does not justify his judgments through a teleological model; his projected sense of world-weariness and detachment is more stoic than utopian. I use him as exemplar for the theme of "criticism" because a concern of his is to undermine the authority of a thesis found in both formalist and intentional aesthetics, namely, the dominance of "author" in interpretation, since this is achieved through a certain collusion with the value "work." As an alternative, Barthes offers a nonauthoritarian aesthetic based on the value of "reader."[22]

Unlike the communally directed ambitions of progress-centered aesthetics, Barthes's "reader" is the singular one of individual sensibility, and aesthetic value is located in autonomous, noncumulative interpretations—or "readings." The thrust of Barthes's critique is modernist to the extent that it embodies the value of protecting autonomy from domination. He perceives the threat as coming from two distinct, but converging, ideological directions: Autonomy is threatened by the persistence of the author's claim to be the voice of the work and the work's claim that its meaning is exhausted when its author's intentions are revealed. The presence of the author makes the work dependent, in that it is formally circumscribed by the sufficiency of that presence. The reader is also dependent, since only those interpretations that are consistent with authorial meaning will do. Thus, although the work shares somewhat in the spoils of domination, neither it nor the reader are autonomous.

There are extra-artistic reasons here for Barthes's dislike of this turn of theory. He locates the presumption of authorial dominance in certain of the theory's social extensions (he calls them "hypostases") that collectively constitute the substratum underlying the concept of author; they are that realm of pre- or nontextual "meanings" that give rise to the degraded species of author as "person." Barthes finds this author-person in the popular media consorting with rock stars and politicians and so exemplifying "the epitome and culmination of capitalist ideology."[23] This alone seems to provide grounds for Barthes critically to call for, or circumspectly to notice, the death of this author. One consequence of the void this death creates is the emergence of a new author, one that Barthes calls a scriptor and locates entirely "within" the text, thereby eliminating the possibility of contamination by hypostasis.

This depersonalization of author into scriptor is evidently to be taken in a positive sense, both socially and aesthetically. But the new entity, bearing as it does a promise of autonomy for another categorial part, the reader, invites some scrutiny. One comparison that suggests itself is with "scribe," the one who writes down what Pharaoh says. These two, scriptor and scribe, share a sense of passivity; the scriptor has no interests to put forth, and the scribe takes care to hide those he may have. But Barthes's scriptor has no Pharaoh, nor is there a suggestion that one will soon appear. If the author-person is the "culmination" of capitalism, is the author-scriptor capitalism's last dregs or the phoenix flower of a new order? I suspect that Barthes thinks the former—for last dregs, like sediment in good wine, can be enjoyed. There is no revolution here, merely what Barthes calls a "bourgeois decomposition," perhaps but another form of progress. The death of the author-person is not sudden; it is a lingering one, a wasting away in which the pretensions of personality come to reveal themselves and then fall off, vitiating the excitement of searching the work for its author.

Another characteristic of both scriptor and scribe, in addition to passivity, is an indifference to the causality connecting source and consequence. "Indifference" is a peculiar version of the "timeless present" and is thus a mark of stoicism, which I suggest typifies Barthes. Stoicism is a philosophy linked to late cultures, and its doctrine of indifference can be seen as a defense against futility. It is a doctrine that one would gladly reject at any prospect of regaining one's own youth, but that one retains if the prospect is only to become as the youths of one's old age actually are. The scriptor, by virtue of depersonalization, is a stoic who has defeated time. For others (the reader perhaps), the decomposition proceeds slowly, and this provides that certain detached "ease" that is Barthes's preferred state. But the scriptor's time is not the "time of one's life" but the time of writing, and, as Barthes puts it: "Every text is eternally written here and now."[24] The scriptor always means what he writes, since he originates with the text. There is nothing, no independent "authorial" meaning, that struggles to be expressed through the text. Writing, meaning, and scriptor are all a fact, indeed, the same fact. The stoic rejects the linkage between possibility and preference; the external world of pity and blame is as much to be avoided as is the internal world of hope and despair. If the stoic is thus indifferent to consequences, there being no good grounds for preferring one to another, so the writing of the scriptor is indifferent to interpretations, for there are no good reasons why any one interpretation should be taken as better than any other.

Because of his assault on intentionality, Barthes has been linked to the late modernist thesis that the author's death corresponds to the critic's birth: "critic as artist," "theory assuming the status of its subject," "language become the world." But I believe this to be wrong—it is too aggressive, too programmatic for Barthes. He defends his autumnal enjoyment against this codification as well. The new collective order in which language would be "exterior, motionless and dogmatic" is also an enemy: language reified, language become Pharoah, the dominance of the work through its emissary, the critic. In the transition Barthes makes from "author" to "scriptor," there is a parallel transition from "work" to "text." As Barthes describes it: "A text is not a line of words releasing a single 'theological' meaning (the message of the Author-God) but a multi-dimensional space in which a variety of writings, none of them original, blend and clash."[25] The author is the "past" of the work; the scriptor is the "present" of the writing. As with all his moves, Barthes does not take this replacement as a victory but as an uncovering. Peeling off the historical layers, what is uncovered is the "reader"—and Barthes makes the further distinction between reader and critic.

The critic is actually child of the author qua "person," and their familial complicity shows a historical progression: In the earlier form, the author, in the fullness of infatuation with self, shapes the extension of life and loves into the intension of the work. Each work holds the author's meaning, or some of it, for there is more in a life than can be compressed into a text. So it is the critic's task to interpret all the texts, the "life's work," to get at the life. But it happens that as author-persons proliferate over time, interest in their lives wanes, and aesthetic value migrates elsewhere. It is then recognized that there is more in a work than can be attributed to its author's life. A new alliance can now be forged between work and critic. But if the critic is indeed the author's issue, there is an inheritance provided: the twin concepts of domination and closure. The ascendancy of the critic over the work is based on the thesis that the value of the work rests in language rather than in its author, and that the determination of such value is the provenance of the critic. This thesis, however, does not undermine the entities involved, it merely transfers power—closure is maintained. So there still are good and bad works, as there were before, but now the critic not only knows but makes the difference. Yet, whether aesthetic value here is construed as "in" a work or as "put in" by the critic, it remains objective and is thus a property of things rather than concepts. As such, it is to be guarded as one does one's other possessions, and this is also the critic's provenance.

Surely, for Barthes, the audience as critic is as much part of the "bourgeois decomposition" as is the author as person, and both need waiting out—not so much to be vanquished as studiously avoided. "Critic" is now replaced with "reader," who joins with the other surrogates, "scriptor" and "text," in a new triad. Barthes offers this triad as one from which all contention, all efforts at domination, have disappeared, for it has the characteristic that its parts, while there for inspection and enjoyment, will merge with each other at the slightest provocation. This, however, seems to deny my earlier proposal: that "reader" is dominant in Barthes's theory. In one sense it is a denial, in the specific sense that Barthes rejects dominance as a relationship and, thus, supervenience as a method. In another sense, however, reading only becomes possible when the concept of "work" expands to include everything that can be read as "text," and that is possible only when texts become actions in the eternal present: "writings." To see the world as text in this inclusive sense is a child's view, and a child's response is play. This is also the reader's response, but it must be properly understood: A child's play is serious; it is not "childsplay," but a response in kind to a world that "has play," a response that puts that world together. Barthes's reader does the same with writing. As Barthes puts it: "The reader is the space on which all the quotations that make up a writing are inscribed without any of them being lost; a text's unity lies not in its origin but in its destination."[26] The notion of a space in which past voices come together is not an image of dominance, but it does contain an ontological claim: Scriptor and writing, in discarding author and work, lose concreteness; in themselves they are little more than judgments on the despotism of their sources. But as inscriptions—as particular readings—they (re)gain the existence that art requires.

5. THE DILEMMA FOR MODERNISM

Barthes's ruminative elitism contrasts with other modernist versions of that time through its lack of ambition. Pace Hegel, things will not get better, and there is no need for acolytes. Offered is not an ideology but a rarified sensibility, of the kind (as with Kant's "genius") that confounds emulation. This is perhaps most galling for the modernist belief in solutions. The usually surmountable hindrances of methodology and style are not even at issue here: How can one ever get to know, for example, when "all the quotations that make up a writing" are present; and if one cannot know, why does one continue to read? The belief in progress could be sustained if one held that interpretations historically accumulate to a point of adequate understanding, that together they exhaust the meaning of a work. But to suggest that, in principle, there is no point of adequacy because all interpretations are autonomous as regards their accumulating fellows is to relinquish the belief in progress. Barthes can be interpreted in this second way.

This poses a dilemma for late modernism: The vaunted principles of form and expression are here criticized as tools of domination, as propaedeutic to social manipulations that wear the masks of "critic" and "author." And criticism itself is compromised, for its new infatuation with power is said to simply facilitate the process of domination and closure. When one interprets this late modernism, against which Barthes's polemics are leveled, as modernism in institutional form, one expects it to react, as institutions are apt to do, with anxiety over such covert operations directed against its own ideological domain. The need for self-protection then becomes evident, and one strategy is to codify the beliefs with which the institution, heretofore, has loosely been identified. As it is the stability of the future (of modernism) that is at risk here, protecting this future can be furthered by specifying the values through which new art is to be characterized, whatever that art turns out to be. Of course, viewed from another vantage point, this inhibits progress—and criticism—for the sake of sustaining modernism. This is belief turned into dogma.

EIGHT

Three Dogmas of Modernism

1. THE VIEW FROM THE PRESENT

THE TERM "postmodernism" is a designator for this time of ours that does not yet have its own name. Whether this tentativeness in naming is a mark of anticipation or of indifference is, like the term itself, not clear. One possibility is that in deference to the accomplishments of our modernist heritage, we feel that the truly new images and doctrines will take time in forming, and that being "post-" is merely to allow ample time for gestation. Others, however, may feel that talk of "anticipation" is nostalgic, perhaps only a eulogy for modernism disguised as a plea for its continuation, and that such talk has no place among the "post-art," "post-history," "post-ideology" values that now (finally) liberate us from the pretensions of our past. Despite these disagreements, however, the partisans on both sides of this question do have something in common: All involved have lived in at least part of modernist history, and few could now say that, all along, they knew that all of it—the proclamations, purifications, instigations, all that glorious reaching—would end so indecisively and so soon. So we are all at some risk here: Those of us who think of the present as a time of collective breath catching between the historical peaks of modernism and post-postmodernism, and those others of us who feel that our future has become a process of endlessly finessing the achievements of the liberated present. The risk is that in the rush to deny our earlier beliefs we may forget why we believed them, why they were so attractive to begin with. Such forgetting makes the denial easier, for it is the kind of historical forgetting that permits us to continue using the vestiges, the moribund images, of these beliefs whenever it suits our needs. This forgetting is also ideologically safe, for the vestiges of belief no longer have the power to demand our allegiance, they merely provide us with security. Yet, paradoxically, through the insistence of their familiar clutter, they do manage to inhibit the formation of beliefs that could move us on.

Actually, the ideological distance between modernism's last days and where we are now may be greater than is readily apparent. This is because the themes of modernist ideology, once so new and demanding, are now both familiar and dispensible, and they influence us more, as do changes in fashion, than changes in conviction. And, as with fashion, there is a good chance that any rejected beliefs, somewhat altered, will reappear and seduce us once again. But it also may be that the easy flow of surface change masks a displacement in more fundamental values, and that we postmodernists may already have ceased to believe what some of us are still willing to entertain.

If we take the position, one that is perhaps itelf a modernist belief, that the past is not only what we have lived through but something we must transcend, then we should identify those aspects of the past we have discarded, even if we may not (yet) know why. My suggestion, around which this chapter develops, is this: If we do not know what postmodernism is, we might help our inquiry by asking what it is not—or not any longer. This would identify the modernist doctrines that have become our present-day dogmas and conceptual constraints.

2. THE NATURE OF DOGMA

The three thematic transformations under discussion here: from "taste" to "form," from "expression" to "intention," and from "progress" to "criticism," have been presented as modernist beliefs that have historical roots in the aesthetic theories of Kant, Schopenhauer, and Hegel. Yet, as this chapter's title indicates, I view these beliefs as having become dogmas of modernism. My reasons for this are also historical: By so recasting these beliefs, I mean to characterize the shift from modernism to postmodernism as first an aquiescence to and then a rejection of dogma. In the final chapter of this study, I present a postmodernism that builds its own identity on the accomplished repudiation of modernist ideology. Here, however, my interest is in describing the process of repudiation that precedes the building. Given this, a closer look at the notion of "dogma" is needed.

A dogma is a belief we continue to sustain for reasons that are mostly irrelevant to what it is we believe. Thus, a dogma is not so much a belief as a posture of prudence—there are perceived benefits in holding on to it. Often, these benefits are simply the comforts of familiarity, or the inertia through which we resist an inchoate future. Indeed, we often blame the future for our present dogmas; we blame it for not revealing itself quickly enough, or for frightening us when it does. To be sure, the transition into postmodernism is not frightening to us as was the advent of modernism; our dogmas have not yet been challenged by unthinkably novel beliefs. But postmodernism has indeed been slow and inconspicuous in its arrival: We scarcely know we are in it or what exactly has changed.

Dogmas are nothing if not practical: They admit as many interpretations as are necessary to cope with events. If the events are acceptable, then the dogmas can be adapted to them. Beliefs, on the other hand, exert pressure on events by distinguishing between those that should be acceptable and those that should not. The beliefs of modernism functioned as polemical weapons in the wars of competing isms—the wars to determine which style truly exemplifies the art and values of modernity. With the advent of postmodernism, the wars are mostly over, but the isms remain, now coexisting in the ideologically opaque context of a market-based relativity. Dogmas, but not beliefs, lend themselves to the statistical manipulation of preference. This, as I note above, is because beliefs become dogmatic when the practical interests they serve replace their need for theoretical justification. So preferences change to fit the evolution of these interests, although the rhetoric of change refers back to the antecedent belief. The difficulty here, both aesthetic and social, is in continuing to use the rhetoric of outmoded beliefs in our attempt to justify present preferences. But the problems with rhetoric are not necessarily problems with art: It is probably excessive at this point to characterize the art of late modernism as dogmatic—or, which is much the same thing, as "academic"—although it does seem to me that artists of the past few years have been particularly vulnerable to social and institutional manipulation.[1] Perhaps one way to explore the view that the decline of modernism is marked by an exploitation of its own achievements is to do as I suggest here, namely, to examine the modernist beliefs that survive as dogma, that have become the sources of postmodern discontent. If we identify what in these beliefs is not cogent, or no longer relevant, then we can better articulate the value framework of today's art, inasmuch as it is highly reactive to these beliefs.

3. "TASTE" TO "FORM" AS DOGMA

I return now to the thematic transition from "taste" to "form." Form, in modernist theory, came to have a double reference: (*a*) to the autonomy and self-referentiality of the tradition of art, and (*b*) to the primacy for interpretation of the formal properties of artworks. This coupling counters the charge that formalism is a parochial ideology relevant only to a limited group of modernist works. The first condition (*a*), gives us the thesis that "art is about art," that, for example, the history of artworks exhibits an internal, quasi-causal development that is explanatory without requiring reference to social origin or function. This, in turn, supports the claim made by (*b*), that what is *aesthetically* important in artworks, form, is a discriminable constant within the entire history of art. This claim does not call for a distinction between "form" and "nonform," for unless restricted to Genesis, such a distinction produces ontological absurdities. But the wanted distinction does separate artistic from nonartistic form and thus authenticates the category "art." Given this authentication, other distinctions can be made concerning the intensity and purity through which formal concerns are demonstrated. These, in turn, provide a basis for value judgments between artworks.

This claim has evident problems, however. To begin with, there is the presumption of ahistoricity: that the formalist thesis holds for all historical art notwithstanding the complicity the thesis has, in both origins and polemical mission, with a certain limited segment of modernism. To counter this, one could argue that art-historical traditions have typically regarded formal characteristics as having instrumental rather than constitutive aesthetic value: "Good form" is not the goal of art, but only the means through which artworks accomplish their larger symbolic tasks, however these are variously construed in given societies. This argument keeps formalism intact, but at the cost of diluting its modernist polemic for "pure form."

A related problem with the formalist view is the assumption that the aesthetic character of art is itself the normative constant in the history of art: that, through all the vagaries of style, the point of art remains the revelation of the subject of "taste." This is the subject Kant assigns to art, and the dependency of formalism on his aesthetic can again be noted on this score. But, as I also note, Kant's concerns are with systematic completeness, and the philosophical use he makes of art is not tied to its history of development. For the presumption that art's true subject, however we define it, exhibits a *historical* constancy, we are indebted, not so much to Kant, but to the thesis I identify as the "Hegelian plateau."[2] This thesis holds that, from the vantage of the present, reason (finally) escapes the relativism of historical position and can see the past as it "really is." The formalist version of this (and its modernist "present" is, of course, later than Hegel's) is that past art of value can now be seen as "really" concerned with the purities of internal structure, despite all that was variously said and how most was used. This thesis does not only apply to past history. The claim of formal primacy extends the Hegelian plateau by holding for the future as well: Future art of value will continue to be that art which is concerned with formal purity, notwithstanding what might later be said or done. I suggest here that it is through this "arrogance of the indubitable present," this unwillingness to contextualize the practice of taste, that the theme "taste" to "form" congeals into dogma.

Symptoms of this dogmatic turn in the formalist thesis can be found in the transition from early to late modernism.[3] The early emphasis on form is replete with attempts to rid art of distractions—to "purify" and "reduce" artistic means to the actuality of self-reference. Mondrian presents his abstract forms and colors as both culmination and essence of pictorial art; Arnold Schönberg conquers diatonic affability by referring all musical sequences to prior constructions of the twelve-tone row; Gertrude Stein elevates sense over reference by forcing what is said back into the saying. In late modernism, however, these positions are subject to a strategy of reversal: Andy Warhol shows us that everything has form, the differences depending on what attracts (first his, then our) attention; John Cage makes music by having us listen to (any) ambient sound for some (arbitrarily given) length of time; and the lyrics of rock indicate that sense is not so much in language as in the subversion of language by its performance.

In all these, the selection of what is taken as "form" is based on considerations that are independent of the sensibility historically associated with good taste. Bell's "significant form" now falls victim to art's new ontological disarray: When interest moves from the autonomy of art to the boundaries between art and non-art, the breakdown in the discriminatory power of the predication " . . . is art" also undermines the authority of form in appreciation. The democratization of the category "art"—as regards its neighbor "non-art"—involves procuring autonomy for both. This results in a peculiar inversion of modernist ideology: Non-art seeks its freedom from the ontological domination of art, from the claim to greater symbolic potency that artistic form has been leveling against its secular counterpart. This claim, secured in large part by formalism, underlies the historical domination of modernism. The aesthetic emancipation of non-art signals the end of that domination.

4. "EXPRESSION" TO "INTENTION" AS DOGMA

The second theme that I follow into its dogmatic turn is in the transition from "expression" to "intention." This theme turns away from the self-referentiality of art and toward the inhibitions that social conventions purportedly impose on our affective responses to the world. Presented as a value, this theme presumes our pervasive unwillingness or inability to feel deeply, and this limitation in our emotional capacity is construed as having epistemic roots, a collective poverty in our knowing what is real. Artistic creativity is the model for overcoming this limitation, a thesis that I have traced to Schopenhauer's artist, who offers us, through works and personal example, the expanded and intensified world we fear to meet directly.

One sign of difficulties with this theme can be found in its overwhelming popular success, especially in late modernism. Theoretically, if looked upon as a basic component of aesthetic value, the creative impulse and its objectification should be style-independent, in the same sense that "form" is viewed as a normative constant within the history of art. But in examining the historical succession of style into the modernist period, it is apparent that this theme correlates better with certain sequences than others: The preoccupation with artistic creativity emerges as a central aesthetic value in nineteenth-century Romantic art and continues through the various Expressionist styles in Europe and, subsequently, in America.[4] Within this succession of styles, the artist's psyche comes to be taken as the glass through which artistic content is to be seen, and the historical progression from the one to the other moves toward the merging—even the identity—of the artist's process and the manifest content of the work.

In the modern period, Expressionist art moved rapidly

from its earlier status of neglect and censorship to cultural preeminence in the museums and concert halls. The early "styleless honesty" of the painfully externalized image soon became the most familiar of styles: Van Gogh's life sparked the occasion for a vast cultural industry of penitence and self-examination, and his replicated self-portraits now look out from above the sofas of countless living rooms. The paintings of Jackson Pollock generated not only thousands of disciples but floor coverings and evening gowns as well. The arduous and self-destructive efforts of the Schopenhauerian genius had become easy to emulate and, in that quintessentially late-modern term, "accessible" to appreciation.

This democratization of the Expressionist ideal has a theoretical side as well. There is an elitism to the early concept of "expression" that is analagous to the one that can be ascribed to "taste." Kant, through the concept of taste, separates the appreciation of beauty from personal inclination. He ties success in this difficult task to the same characteristic, the capacity to "universalize," that he requires for the developed moral disposition. While, in theory, this is the characteristic he holds to be common to all rational beings, in practice it is associated with a relatively few cultivated individuals.[5] The capacity for "good taste," then, is both socially elitist and a theoretical condition of aesthetic appreciation. The sublimation that aesthetic taste demands from the individual, the ability to withstand the superficial gratifications of mimesis and narrative, also supports the propensity to identify form as the central aesthetic value.

Expression, in its popular sense, is scarcely to be associated with sublimation—quite the contrary. But it also has elitist origins that, like those of form, can be located in the rejection of superficiality. Looking back to the pairing of the Kantian "sublime" with Schopenhauer's "will," one can trace this exclusiveness to the notion of magnitude: The expressive artist probes "deeper," the world revealed is "richer," and its significance "greater." Expression is identified with a certain manner and content the absence of which, as in the case of the "ordinary" individual, is identified with a *lack of* expressiveness. The thesis of "intentionality," that to find out what an artwork means, one has to discover what the artist intended it to mean, need not be associated with the value of expression: If intentions are revelatory of artistic meanings in general, they must have other vehicles besides "feelings." However, when intentions and feelings *are* joined together, an event I locate in modernism, then the status of expression as an aesthetic value is historically strengthened. But given the elitist cast of its origins, in "genius" and "sublimity," this value cannot be found in every work and any artist. Rather, the question must be asked, Which intentions are worth pursuing? Out of the many, which few will reveal to us a way of being in the world we could not otherwise know? The "infection" transmitted by Tolstoi's artist is not merely something that entertains us, but something we need; we do not follow the rocky road from expression to intention only to reach a facsimile of our own unremarkable existence.

Now, what eventually comes to confront this belief is the contrary belief that, barring considerations of manner and style, we all express ourselves all the time, and that attempts to normatively differentiate between expressions are all forms of elitism and, thus, of domination. This second belief can be given some perspective by considering the demographic changes in the status of the artist during the period in question.

The inception of modernism separated "advanced" artists from the residual academics—a further splintering away from an already small professional group. The ethos of the event centered on the change in how artistic activity is construed: the change from "vocation" to "calling." Under this latter usage, the term "professional artist" becomes an oxymoron: Artists "have to do" what they do, and matters of professional success are of little importance. This is the familiar ethos of the artist as bohemian. Paradoxically, in the transition to late modernism, this ethos, the image of restrictive high-seriousness, became so popular as to extend the study of art from the academy into general education. This identification of art *practice* as one among the many subjects to be studied in the primary and secondary schools gave rise to a considerable postwar industry in education, which grew even larger with studio art's new respectability on the university level in the liberal arts curriculum. Given this democratization and the numbers involved, inculcating the values of creativity and self-expression also became the provenance of general education.[6]

General acceptance of these values, however, required some modifications in belief. Evidently, if the benefits of creativity are for all to sample, they must first be demystified. This is another way of saying that the various beliefs supporting exclusiveness in the arts must be reexamined and, in all likelihood, rejected. The value of "expression," which, through inheritance, contains a number of such (atavistic) beliefs, must be updated: The first belief to go is about the rarified nature of genius—that, since only a few have the capacity to produce great works, only they should aspire to do so. The second dispensable belief identifies creativity with illness—the picture of the artist as maladjusted and self-destructive. The third such belief asserts the primacy of value judgments in interpretation—the belief that only good art is valuable.

The counters to these beliefs can be put in the following ways: First, we are, as it turns out, all creative. This refers back to the concept of "genius," and what it denies is not the concept as such, the fact that in given fields there are people with surpassing abilities, but the premise that this is a regulative concept for the practice of art. The coupling of creativity with genius is replaced by its coupling with success at popularity. The counter to the second belief holds that making art is salutory for everyone. Here the reference is to the construal of artist as victim, the association of self-destructiveness and social marginality with creativity. The denial of this thesis is consequent on a developing pluralism in society, where individual subjectivity is no longer taken as a threat to social order. This is supported by the new socially integrative view of art making where, on sum, the subjectivities of a reasonably content citizenry would produce little that might be so extraordinary as to be socially threatening. The counter to the third belief holds that the value of creativity is attested to by process, not product. The target here is the dominance of normative judgments in art theory, the presumption that the history of art is *consequentially* a history of masterworks. "Genius" is a rare and solitary bird. The communality of art making is threatened by this presumption because, under it, products of a mass creativity would be counted as having little artistic value. Rejecting this presumption entails rejecting the hold that history exerts on practice. When we do this, we come to view the creating of artworks as also a creating of the conditions of their history and value. These conditions are quite different from the ones that support the value an artwork seeks when it is a supplicant within the history of art. In a pluralistic community of artistic expression, the narrative of an artwork's making provides the history that counts.[7]

The democratization of art implied by each of the above points can be considered an attack on the values of modernism, and the called-for "demystification" of artistic expression, a sign of postmodernism. Both, in effect, recognize art's new entry into mass culture through its rejection of the normative coupling of expression and high art—another of the modernist beliefs turned dogma.

5. "PROGRESS" TO "CRITICISM" AS DOGMA

The last theme I wish to follow into its dogmatic turn is the transition from "progress" to "criticism." Of the three discussed here, this theme is actually the hardest to give up. Although we may accept its exhaustion in the aesthetic world, many of us would like to retain its viability for other, political and social, spheres. Within the polemics of modernism, an artist's dependency on antecedent historical forms is viewed as a regression—a loss of nerve that devalues the work whatever its other merits may be. In fact, it is specifically these other merits, the ingratiations of medium and subject found in premodern art, that are most suspect here, for they support the values of class and privilege at which the critical aspect of the new art is leveled.

The postmodernist may no longer believe that art progresses when progress is viewed as an inexorable "purification" of form and content, and the artwork as a finger pointed by an impatient future at a recalcitrant public. But there is some currency left in the notion that our culture is, must be, getting better at coping with its problems. Surely art must still have some part in this, if no longer as a goad, at least as a witness.

I suggest that the theme of "progress to criticism" has not totally followed modernism into the historical past. It is not as easily upended as were the other two. One reason is that, unlike the others, this theme lacks determinate content: Any particular formal or affective characteristic wanted for a new art can be given up and the proposition that that art exemplifies progress still maintained. These theoretical descriptions of linkages between past and future are not only causal but normative as well. In the same sense that arriving future events can invariably be shown to be consequent on some aspect of the past, so can the latest symbols be shown to be some kinds of improvements on earlier ones. The present state of affairs, the art of today, need not make this seem counter-intuitive: It should be remembered that, in high modernism, the formal parsimony of artworks was often regarded as a sign of progress, and their obscurity a sign of their critical prowess. But, of course, we must now find our own signs. We can no longer use the formal imperatives of modern artworks, nor can we accept the social dictates of the artistic avant-garde. The reason for this, as I point out in the preceeding discussions, is not that these signs have become foreign and opaque to us; to the contrary, they are now so familiar that they no longer provide us with the clues to "exemplary novelty" that we need.

The theme of progress is the administrator of modernist ideology; it derives specific content from attenuated interpretations of the other themes. When the concept of form is so historicized that past art is only for vanquishing but never for returning to, then progress assumes the cloak of "inevitability" and presents itself as the doctrinal arbiter of the future. When the concept of expression is differentiated through its contrast with the sentiments of the "unfeeling bourgeoisie," then progress maintains its authority through the politics of class warfare. The concept of progress, when it turns into modernist dogma, remains unremittingly teleological. Its goal is clear in principle even though its articulations may be opaque in practice. Its success is based on the premise that recalcitrant artists, deviant styles, and restless audiences will all be overcome through the inevitable dialectic closure.

The dilemma that arises at this point, one that can be traced back to the Hegelian thesis of the "end of art," is that the telic goals of modernism, once reached in consciousness and artistic form, leave little more for the artist to do.[8] Here is where the dogma emerges: The residue of modernist ambitions insists that the goals have not yet been reached and, marked by accusation and counteraccusation, the succession of stylistic isms accelerates, each claiming centrality in the progress of "progress." Continuing belief in "inevitability" is the now debilitating constant—the belief turned dogma.

The rejection of Hegelian historicism is a rejection of the belief that a predictive pattern can be imposed on (more benignly, "found in") history and then used to justify social practice. The correlate in aesthetics would be a rejection of the belief that a predictive pattern, one that takes a historical virtue and uses it in the assignment of value to new art, can be imposed on stylistic change. These rejections bring welcome relief, not the least of which is freedom from the sheer weight of ideology, but they also create some new anxieties. The time of modernism, for all its rhetoric of "autonomy," was actually quite puritanical—history replacing divinity as the warning finger shaken at the artist. With the restrictions gone, however, and the seductions of a suddenly "neutral" history now open to art, there seem not to be any good reasons to choose one way rather than another.

A major anxiety of postmodernism is that its art has largely become a hedonic index, where economic justification replaces ideological justification. Of course, it can be argued that the opening of art to the symbolic, and practical, needs of the greater society does achieve the long-desired social integration of art. But against this, it can also be argued that this integration may now be too complete, for art is taking on some of society's bad habits. In this uncertain climate, the critical function of art—a mainstay, after all, of modernist ideology—is increasingly difficult to maintain. One might darkly conjecture here that the "fact" that art is no longer very important may, paradoxically, be a sign of its further progress. But this gloom can be lightened by the conjecture that art's lack of importance may now be the criticism art levels at the dogma that it is important. Both these conjectures belong to postmodernism.

6. ALTERNATIVES

My discussions throughout this chapter are based on a common contention: that one way to understand postmodernism is to ask what it is about modernist values that makes us uncomfortable. The answers I give in these discussions suggest a new question: With what have we replaced these values? In comparing the two periods, one notes a conspicuous absence of doctrinal concern in today's art. Postmodernism has been accused of replacing the aesthetic, and social, goals of modernism with fragmented and expedient strategies; and the cheerful permissiveness of our art world has been characterized as only an attempt to suppress the anxieties evoked by the critical part of modernism and our failure to cope with its demands. Of course, these accusations can themselves be attacked as modernist nostalgia. But it does seem that the political and social events of our present time are a good deal more radical than our art: Our world seems to have outrun its symbols or, at least, some things we have been accustomed to valuing as symbols. These difficulties may indeed portend the eventual emergence of a new high style—a renaissance that both sums up the second half of the twentieth-century and sets up the artistic concerns of the twenty-first. This eventuality would indeed be welcome, but believing in it may only be a corrosive remnant of Hegelian "inevitability," one that does not provide the present with either programs or good reasons for action. If so, the testing of other beliefs is warranted.

I suggest that the modernist dogmas inherited by postmodernism depend, for their continuing credibility, on the presumption of a unified realm of art. It may be, however, that the difficulties these dogmas expose indicate that the category "art" has become too diffuse and unwieldy: It now contains so many incommensurables that it can no longer sustain, nor can we make collective sense of, all that goes on in its name. But this dilemma could, in fact, conceal a creative opening: Setting aside the many evocations the term "art" now inspires—from the conceits through the humilities—we might seek to dismantle the category, not in favor of a new competitor, but to so disarrange and scatter the theoretical compliants of ". . . is art," that the new sortings will separately have to find the practices to which they apply. If there are such practices to be found, however inhospitable they may be to being joined under the rubric of "art," then the three themes I have traced into their dogmatic impasse could regain some explanatory power.

I propose here that postmodernism can first be understood as an inversion of modernism—as a denial of the values that "taste," "expression," and "progress" have accumulated in their historical journey. Tracing this denial into its strategies of opposition, its works and ideologies, can then permit a more positive characterization of that period. I conclude my study with such a tracing.

NINE

The Postmodern Legacy

1. THE CLASS OF ARTWORKS

WHEN the distinction between art and non-art is made *within* the concept of art, its strategic force is directed at an epistemic and normative reorganization, but it remains ontologically benign; the concept itself is not challenged. However, in the climate where artistic attention moves from the center to the borders of art, and artists' enthusiasms wax over the fragility of these borders, we might no longer know which parts of the world sustain or merit artistic attention, or even what form such attention should take. Still, we do know that some parts and not others are at issue at any given time. The class "all and only artworks" emerges here as a topological form, in theory compatible with other comprehensive classes, for example, "artifacts," "candidates," "conventionals," but in practice preserving its identity *qua class* by the historical sequestering of its members.[1] We may know that, in principle, there are no distinctions between artworks and other things that can forever withstand artistic ambition, but we continue to make such distinctions for the sake of the unity of the concept. This unity has often been characterized by the phrase "system of the arts," which, in addition to distinguishing between artworks and everything else, implies a functional compatibility between the various arts.[2] This thesis of compatibility has a historical thrust that not only supports cross-realm comparisons of value and style but also sanctions new hybrids, for example, Calder's kinetic sculptures and Jasper Johns's paintings of words, on the presumption that such new forms elaborate but do not threaten the essential unity of the system. Thus, through the thesis that the term "art" designates a particular class or system, we protect the thesis that all the various arts share certain characteristics that are both individually constitutive and constitutive for the class. Whatever these characteristics are, and even if they cannot, or can no longer, be specified, we count them as constitutive so as to preserve the class and, thereby, the autonomy of art. Of course, classes—classically defined—are eternal and do not need us to "preserve" them. We, on the—also classical—other hand, are obligated to identify them as best we can. Accepting this obligation reveals the staying power, however attenuated, of our faith in the theoretical endurance of the class "all and only artworks," despite our historically contingent inability to always distinguish it from other classes. Keeping such faith has its rewards: To conceive of art in this way protects it, and us, from uses to which it might otherwise be put and company it might otherwise keep.

These days, taking artworks to constitute a class, rather than a logically weaker aggregate of historical artifacts and events, requires us to argue in either of two ways. These arguments are quite different, especially when they are used to predict art's future, but they have in common an attitude toward our present that is marked, respectively, by impatience or disdain: We can argue that our postmodern problems with the constitutive characteristics of artworks are merely a fin de siècle exhaustion brought about by excessive theorizing—one that, in good time, will be remedied by a new high style; or we can argue that the class "art" is historically complete, that the possibility of making new (bona fide) artworks is past—and that, in any case, there are no longer any good reasons to do so. This second is essentially the thesis of "the end of art."

I shall not comment much on the argument supporting the anticipation of a new high style. My reasons for this are largely aesthetic. There is an troublesome complacency and inertia to this argument that dooms its advocates to experiencing the present by avoiding it, or, less iconoclastically, to searching a hostile terrain for a glimpse of something familiar and comforting, for variations on novel form and individual expression. Either way, this is the argument of academic modernism.

The second argument, suggesting the "end of art," is more rewarding.[3] It provides a finale to the modernist theme of "progress" to "criticism," and it also revives the Hegelian notion of art's eventual exhaustion as a symbolic form. In Chapter Eight, I suggest that one sign of the transition from modernism to postmodernism is the claim that art is no longer important. No modernist, as a participant in that time, would then have accepted the claim that art is unimportant, but now, as a survivor, might very well admit—even revel in the fact—that it has become so.

One must ask, of course, how this claim slices history: Is it directed merely at present practice, or at the whole of tradition? Actually, the two do not separate neatly, although the former may have greater present urgency. The claim that our art is unimportant may be taken in the benign sense that it is "post-art." And this, in turn, may indicate that we are well rid of "importance," and all those world-historical postures and iconographic ambitions the term implies. However, the claim may also be taken pejoratively to mean that present art is not a symbol but only a symptom of culture; and, as such, it no longer has claim to special value or even unity. The tension between these interpretations—the play between art's end, its aftermath, and its importance—calls for a critique of that theory of art from which it derives.

2. POST-ART ART

Art construed as "system of the arts" peaks in modernism in the guise of society's universal corrective. Its comprehensive message is seen as relevant to all groups, in all aesthetic and social efforts that are directed at emancipation from the past. When the system fails, when art "degenerates" into piecemeal affinities with particular interest groups, when commonality of interest as expressed by formal and stylistic coherence is lost, then art ends. Art that cannot sustain a unified teleology loses symbolic importance for the goal of that teleology. Under this view, postmodern art is not art because the many things now called art show no interest in historical coherence; each activity has its own imperatives. From the modernist perspective the class is then historically closed.

One way of dealing with this "end of art" argument is by affirming it, but in the benign sense indicated above of "Who cares?" This is probably the majority view among today's practitioners who are bored enough by modernist dogmatics to simply dismiss them. But the theoretical counter to this argument is more elusive, for it entails showing that the modernist conflation of historical finality and formal unity is flawed. In this regard one could argue, for example, that the unity of the arts presumed by the end-of-art thesis is a relatively recent phenomenon—having arisen in the Renaissance in response to a realignment between the guilds of artisans and professionals—but that its usefulness is now itself at an end. The unity of art thus joins company with the other theoretical unities: one-world society, unity of science, et cetera, whose use is now largely ceremonial and pietistic.[4] This argument further indicates that "art" is now only an honorific term and that concern about art's end is nothing but apprehension about the social consequences of losing the distinction between artworks and things that are not art.

Before pressing this issue further, it might be useful to review the stages of discussion thus far. The distinction between art and non-art is supported by the themes whose early appearance I identify as "taste," "expression," and "progress." In the context of the philosophical system to which each theme belongs (respectively, that of Kant, Schopenhauer, and Hegel) each is assigned a specific and unique cognitive function, and performance of this function entails not only the unity of the aesthetic realm the theme describes but the unity of the larger system as well. The transition of these themes into their modernist versions: "form," "intention," "criticism," carries with it the earlier support for the art–non-art distinction. Here, the notion of aesthetic unity is translated into the one of artistic autonomy. Although art now requires the safeguard of its autonomy in order to remain unified, this unity is now justified by art's extrasystematic role as prophet, purifier, and intensifier of social process. The theoretical cogency of this role declines in the late stages of modernism, but the practical urgency invested in it lingers on, and the "end of art" thesis takes on the hyperbolic implications of the "end of an epoch." The nostalgic backlash that greets this latter end can then be used to justify continued allegiance to the aesthetic themes of modernism, and the result is what I describe as their "dogmatic turn."

This returns to the notion that begins this section, the notion that art has ended and that what continues as art is no longer important. The crucial assumption here is that the value of artistic progress only applies when the various arts are conceived as exhibiting a formal, affective, and critical unity. So conceived, the "end of art" is an inevitable, and theoretically welcome, response to present inadequacy, to categorical indifference. This response affirms that although the concept "art" no longer applies to present practice, the class of all and only artworks remains intact. We are then left with the satisfaction of possessing what that class contains. The problem of what follows, as it is less important, is left to others.

That "what follows" should be a problem at all is because what it contains does not seem to fit anywhere. Post-art artworks do not fit the concept of art because they do not participate in the documentation of the process that closes that concept. They seem unwilling to respond with the proper dignity to an epoch's end. It does seem a shame that this end was not arrived at as the dramatic finale of a latter day *Gesamtkunstwerk,* or even through a minimal—but pervasive—"ping" in some appropriate place. In fact, late modernism has taken a good deal more time than we would theoretically have assigned the end of art; its lingering is somewhat on the model of Zeno's paradox, where the halvings of the distance to be covered, if we let them, continue on no matter how little remains. Art finally ends, then, not because it has reached its end, but because to continue the process of its ending had become an unutterable bore.

Post-art art is not boring. But it remains vulnerable to the attempt by the coalition devoted to art's ending to say what part of it may still be art, thus salvaging a modicum of past importance for a bit of present practice. This attempt may itself be boring, but it is manipulative as well, for its restrictiveness is directed more at the reasons for making new art than at the works themselves. Post-art art looks much like art, in fact, like many different kinds of art; but, importantly, the various reasons for making these various kinds seem to have little to do with the reasons associated with art's historical presumptions of unity and autonomy. Here we come closer to the heart of things: Post-art art is unimportant because its reasons deny its autonomy. Its "central" aesthetic virtues do not dominate—indeed, cannot be located in—its various uses. Indeed, there is no common criterion of aesthetic virtues that applies, nor, as it seems, is one wanted. Of the many current things and activities that, if one were still so motivated, might be categorized as art, it seems evident that, unlike a unified art, they have more in common with other things than they do with each other. The "affordable art" of the junk-mail circular does not recognize the graffiti on subway cars, and neither has met the artwork that "just is" the festivities of its opening. Yet they all cohabit in the art of postmodernism.

3. PROGRAMS OF POSTMODERNISM

By now, the period of postmodernism has a history and programs of its own; it is no longer merely a first reaction to the exhaustion of modernism. In its earliest stages, postmodernism was indeed reactive: It evidenced shock at the rapid tumbling of modernist idols and responded with a mix of helplessness, cynicism, and avarice to the "free play of market forces" in the arts. In its later development, what I take to be the present situation, some theoretical strands specific to postmodernism have emerged.

One consequence of the assault on the concept of the unity of art is a questioning of the bases that have supported the system of art history. In this area, revisionist tendencies move more slowly than in the area of practice; whatever our attitudes, the problem of sorting out the art of the past, of rethinking the historical construction of categories, does not disappear. Post-historical revisionism still requires *some* version of history.

Art history, as is evident, is not a comprehensive history of past art; rather, it is of art that is of the kind to be historical. The selectivity is normative. It follows that all art taken as historical is artistically valuable in some agreed-on sense of "value," and is therefore de facto unified under that system of the arts. What changes between modernism and postmodernism is that, increasingly, both the grounds and the very authenticity of this sorting process are questioned. Art history, stripped of its presumptions of unity and exclusivity, not to say teleology, opens to conflicting attitudes on what makes art valuable. The attitudes that have long dominated, that underlie the chosen criteria for historical art, are then seen to mirror the social attitudes exemplified by the very art that is chosen, the art that has survived the historical sorting. There is ample room for revisionist rumblings here: "Attitudes" quickly become redefined as "prejudices," and the history of the "system of the arts" increasingly finds itself defending the normative, now read as "repressive," reasons behind its patterns of exclusion and inclusion. Those aspects of artworks that were previously regarded as "extra-aesthetic"—signifiers of attitudes toward the ideologies of class, sex, race, et cetera—now become central in the new judgments. In keeping with this revisionist thrust, a new, distinctly postmodern attitude toward art history emerges. This is an attitude at once of co-optation and disavowal: Past art is for using, not venerating; it contains no telic imperatives of stylistic transformation or continuity, but it does provide a practical resource for present purposes. The history of art is viewed here as a loose aggregate of artifacts and commentaries whose individual values are functions of their usefulness in present art making. Shifts in these values are not fine-tunings of an inherited historical schema; rather, they exemplify the interdependency of aesthetic judgments and social interests—how needs arising from the latter affect our estimate of the former. Viewed this way, the history of art is only incidentally a history of masterpieces and near misses, for in that guise it primarily concerns the limited world of curators and their constituencies. More interestingly, it is a history of recurring images, contrasting ideologies, and assumable techniques.

In postmodernism, popularity is considered an aesthetic virtue, and popular art, typically, is the art we best remember. What we best remember, then, is not the "best" art, but the best presentations of art—that art which through its exhibitions, performances, reproductions, is most strongly and convincingly impressed upon us. This equation of value and popularity is, of course, a modernist anathema, and if we were to take refuge in, say, the venerable imperatives of "good taste," we would resist the pressures of media, even when guilelessly presented as entertainment or, altruistically, as education. As modernists we would then be free to seek that art which, despite present clamors, remains part of the historically unified whole to which a historically constant standard of value can be applied. But this allegiance to historical norms has the curious consequence that works within this whole, given the "autonomy of art," are more familiar to each other than they are to even the most finely honed of tastes. The society of artworks, under this reading, determines the society of appreciators. Our efforts to enter this circle of familiarity—our own willingness to be so determined—signals our acceptance of the implications of an autonomous art. These implications are political as well as aesthetic.

One thesis that surfaces in postmodernism is the emphasis on the political nature of preference: that motives of persuasion and control underlie *all* efforts to influence preference and taste; neither the "being" nor the "goodness" of art is immune to politics. Although this thesis is not particularly remarkable or novel, it did not surface in modernism, because politics there is identified either with ideality or with coercion. Yet, the construal of art as a *form* of politics, while it entered our beliefs with little theoretical fanfare, has become a postmodern truism. Its acceptance offers a new alternative for appreciation that redirects the scrutiny of artworks away from their formal, affective, and telic characteristics to attitudes these works generate about issues of present political urgency. It is in *this* context that the history of art can also be seen as a history of prejudice, of commission and ommission, as regards the claims of various social groups. It is also in this context that these, often competing, claims are seen as the proper content and justification for postmodern art.

The thesis that the value of art is a distinctly *aesthetic* value is supported by the thesis that artistic autonomy is achieved through a "disinterestedness" in favor of the purely aesthetic. Here, the disturbing factors in past art—the patriarchal commissions and racial ommissions, the various glorifications of class and creed—are regarded as incidental to proper appreciation because art, as art, is not *consequentially* about these but, rather, about its internal, aesthetic, accomplishments. In the postmodernist rejection of this thesis, on the other hand, received art history is characterized as anything but apolitical. Rather, this thesis is viewed as providing covert support for just those political implications in artworks that are overtly described as aesthetically incidental.

The "autonomy of art" thesis, in order to be theoretically cogent, requires the companion thesis that aesthetic value has a single *form* of determination that holds for the entire realm. Specifically, this indicates that, since variations within each particular art do not compromise the validity of uniform judgments, so variations between the arts do not compromise that validity: Some paintings, for example, are better than others, and some poems are better than some paintings.

Actually, this thesis is more exclusionary than inclusionary, for it underlies the distinctions that separate out the consequential arts from all the rest. Thus we arrive at the familiar pairings: art that is high and low, fine and commercial; art and craft, art and kitsch, art for history and art for fun, and so on. The first term in each pair refers to those works brought together under a common judgmental framework; the second term refers to, well, to everything else. Of course, this categorical sequestering can be justified through the Hegelian contention that certain forms, at certain times, have a more consequential symbolic mission than do others. It can also be taken as class warfare, a denigration of certain forms because of origins, audience, and, increasingly, manifest content.

The postmodern interest in the political character of artworks is not directly comparable to the critical stance found in early modernism. The most obvious difference is the present disavowal of the telic ideal of "progress," and the corresponding lack of interest in the strategic value of "universality." Postmodern art is political in the expedient present. It sacrifices the aloofness that preserves aesthetic identity in order to exemplify the attitudes and claims of particular groups. Unlike the anxieties of modernism, postmodern art has no shame; it is complacently instrumental and openly eclectic: Any forms and procedures, from any source, are open to adoption or, more belligerently, co-optation. Some of this has to do with the post-art status of its art: Once denied membership in the community of art-as-art, there is no a priori reason to seek special affinities with any particular members of that community. Here, the historicist view of the development of style is discarded along with the unity-of-art thesis. The art-political urgencies in the postmodern world are immediate ones. Choices are not justified by the promise of their confirmation in a future "high style" but by their promise for manipulating the present. Accordingly, there is no privileged style—no sequence of "begats"—that has priority as a source for new works, and the very notion of "source" becomes democratized as the past loses its linear connection with the present. Thus, historical style becomes a bazaar of available influences: Each present impulse locates the influences that fit, each generates its own tradition and, when the need arises, fashions a supporting ideology.

Distinctions between fine and popular art lose credibility in postmodernism because they are seen more as fostering politically suspect illusions than worthy ambitions. The rejection of these distinctions signals the bankruptcy of the view that art history reveals a pattern of development through which intimations of the future can be spotted in the present. But the rejection also has political roots: denial that appeal to these distinctions will accomplish anything that is of importance for the present. On a different interpretation, this denial is said to underwrite what has been called our "social illiteracy," and is given responsibility for a good part of our national malaise.[5]

In retrospect, the programs of modernism can also be seen as revisionist; but, in contrast with postmodernism, they are more optimistic: modernism, in effect, had to free history from the hesitations of culture so that it could become a true account of social process, thereby opening the possibility for social progress. And avant-garde artworks, through their deliberate provocations, their formal and intentional "purifications," were given the mandate to provide this account. History needed more rather than less attention.

Postmodernism, in contrast, diminishes the role of history; its aims are pluralistic, immediate, and concrete. Its art has no avant-garde; and postmodern artworks, consequently, are eclectic, expedient, and, in the main, ingratiating as a matter of strategy. They resist identification with the category "art" because inclusion in that category, by now, shows a history of constraints rather than opportunities. Consequently, relations between the specific arts are a matter of expedient alliances rather than ideological commonality. In postmodernism, the arts are unified only in the sense that they show a pervasive unwillingness to interpret any sequence of changes as a style that has claim on their collective allegiance.

4. THE AESTHETIC THEMES OF POSTMODERNISM

The thematic transition that is the subject of this study has been presented as a historical and conceptual path that leads from its origins in the late eighteenth century, through its dogmatic turn in late modernism, and into the thematic inversions that mark the beginnings of postmodernism. I conclude my study by tracing the path of each theme a little further: beyond these postmodern beginnings and into the less reactive characteristics of present identity.

Form and Postmodernism Formal attenuation is at least a necessary condition for artistic excellence in modernism. The reductions and purifications of artistic syntax aim at a precision in the identity of art whether the syntactic origins are located in natural phenomena or in the imagination. Nothing that is surplus is tolerated, however much such elements, disparaged as "decorative," might contribute to the ingratiations needed for an equally disparaged version of popular success. As the audience of modern art is art itself, such art does not require external introductions to its content. Modernist reductionism aims at the center of art in the belief that the simple is also the essential.

The postmodernist attack on this principle begins with the suspicion that simplicity is rather at the border of art, for artistic simplicity, particularly when it is repeated, is difficult to distinguish from the horde of simples that begin the realm of nonart: Simplicity as purity dissolves into simplicity as generality. When the forms of excellence are thus mimicked by the forms of the commonplace, the borders of art-as-form, to avoid being shattered, become diffuse. Arthur Danto, in his parable of the "red squares," presses the distinction between "being about nothing" and "not being about anything," the first inviting fullness of content, the second revealing emptiness.[6] The purifications and reductions of Malevich, Mondrian, Reinhardt, are of the first kind—full of nothing but (or as) "spirit" or "essence" or "just art." The painter Robert Rauschenberg, in 1953, tested this austere last row of defenses with a show of blank canvases—which were not about anything. The show itself, being about that, was, of course, not empty. But the boundaries between art and nonart had become diffuse.

There is another direction of assault on formalist values that has a longer history than the one concerned with emptying nothing. By its very nature it is more juicy than the first, for it is more about propriety than ontology. Its target is the social dignity that accompanies historically justified categories, such as the notion of "fine" and "high" in art, and its weapons are the incongruities and images of middle-class commerce. The most familiar examples of this ancestor of postmodernism are found in the provocations of Dada, of Duchamp and his circle, and of American pop art. In each of these, the attack is against a certain alliance between institutional ideals and artistic practices: the presumption that both national policies and artistic styles have a basis in rationality, the collusion between the aesthetics of taste and social stratification, and the exclusion of banality and moral indifference from the content of art. Yet, in each instance, the field of action remains the world of art, and care is taken not to so merge the artwork with the origins of its provocative content that the whole thing is mistaken for a mere "category mistake"—or a disturbance of the peace. It would not do, for example, if the Dadaists were really taken for anarchists or madmen, for then their disturbances would be summarily dealt with and noted in passing by the daily paper. Duchamp, also, did not hide in the Louvre past closing then to draw the mustache on the Mona Lisa—that would merely have been the defacement of a national treasure. Instead, he drew it on a postcard facsimile and the ontology of art was never the same. And Warhol could have exhibited actual Brillo boxes, full of Brillo, instead of the crudely made, hand-painted, "empty," plywood replicas he did use. But if he had done that, it could also have been an error in shipping. These works are all provocations directed at the concept of art, and they all take place within the time of art, albeit with its end in sight. During such time, as it seems, art that seeks to undermine art must do so dependently—as art.

In the postmodernism of the present, when the end of art has come and gone, the gestures of popular art no longer constitute a provocation of mainstream ideology; they become a mainstream of another kind. They form a loose aggregate of images and actions that are "popular," that exemplify the interests of various social groups. These groups, in turn, are identified as the sources of these images, and the competition between artworks is directed toward the authentication of image as (truly) belonging to source. This is the social version of the Expressionist search for origins. The distinction between fine and popular art loses credibility here not only because it is artificial but because it is seen as an aesthetic gerrymandering that generates social categories contrary to the interests of their members.

Popular art, under scrutiny, is not homogeneous; it is not merely that ahistorical "other" of fine art—entities that are so categorized because they are all inconsequential. What binds the popular arts together is not their presumed normative poverty, nor is it their formal similarity. Unlike the fine arts, they do not present common characteristics to which our attention "ought" to be directed; rather, they severally exert pressures in order to *claim* our attention. Here, the history of style is coupled with new technologies of persuasion, to become the general store that caters to all artistic needs. But differences in style do not distinguish between the arts of postmodernism; what does is the social interests to which these arts refer.

Form has no face in postmodernism; there is no formalist imperative that might serve as a taskmaster for other styles. There are, in fact, no distinct styles in postmodernism and, therefore, no need for taskmasters. The impetus in postmodernism is combinatory, and the ensuing combinations are too transient to be fixed as styles. No sooner does an image surface than it is contextualized with other, invariably contrasting, images. The newest media techniques combine with the immediacy of theater and the mediations of the studio arts in the creation of images. The sources of these images are in the commercial and regional arts as well as the fine arts, and the rules governing the cohesion of their forms are as democratic as they are impermanent—"consistency" has become irrelevant. Postmodern works are also more cheerfully expendable than their modernist predecessors: As their ambitions are more political than historical, they have relinquished the internalizing agenda of style, the preoccupation of style with its own continuity. The claims that postmodern works make on our attention correlate with their roles in turning the interests of their origins into our interests, and these origins are often class, race, and gender specific. Successful works seldom survive the objectives at which they are directed; they are unabashedly objects of consumption and, as such, their success lies in our having consumed them, for this is our acknowledgment of the interests they represent.

Postmodern works move through the world with the pace of political programs. They do not engage in the heroics of their social neglect, for memories of the late modernist collusion between the heroic and the sentimental are still fresh. The new formal reality is also a political one: Strategies for combining images from improbable sources into a synthesis can also be used in transforming a polyglot audience into a constituency. As in politics, the value of appreciation is measured quantitatively and, thus, variations in tastes must be satisfied and jaded tastes guarded against in the attempt to find common ground.

In postmodern art, as in its politics, interest is provoked and sustained through an amalgam of novelty and nostalgia, which functions to leaven the unexpected with evocations of the past. This interplay purports to assure us, given the void created by our disavowal of historical teleology, that the form of the future will not be irrational or overly uncomfortable. Postmodern art has often been construed as "eclectic" or "manneristic." These tendencies can be better understood as the attempt to codify a newly inchoate future through a revived focus on memory. The images of memory are found through our new predilections for rummaging—in the archives of historical style, among our personal mementos, and among the artifacts, relics, novelties, and discards of the at-large social production of images. In this way, much like flipping between television channels with our handy "remote," we form novel constellations that, nevertheless, equate the possible with variations on the familiar. The increased range of channels offered by cable television does not (as a modernist might want) offer each of us a choice of sanctuary from the tastes of others. Rather, it enables us to view all tastes as our own, ours being a self-selected proportion of all the others. These amalgams of the familiar—time slices (pace Carnap) of baseball, Bible study, news and romance, even symphony broadcasts and animals in the wild—maintain their interest through the endless variations we command at the press of a finger. We are each a Magister Ludi, finding our novelty in our memories.[7] Through this panorama of images, we reconstitute a past for a culture that, until recently, has had little need for one. And with this newly imaged past, we form a replacement for a future that, bereft of "progress," no longer has a face. The charge of recidivism, which, in modernist times, is leveled against artistic infatuation with the past, has no place in postmodernism.

Intention and Postmodernism Given my general thesis, it seems plausible that the revision in formal values occurring in postmodernism would require commensurate changes in the construal of artistic creativity. The modernist focus is on the expressiveness of the individual artist, and appreciation follows the formal evidence of expressiveness to its source in the artist's intentions. These values evoke an old Aristotelian issue, for we view what this source provides, the circumstances of the hero's downfall, with a mixture of pity and fear. But in the modernist context, the sentiments are not directed at the fictional characters of the drama but at the artist: pity for the psychic cost the artist pays in the effort at reaching and objectifying the sources of expression, and fear of the social cost this effort would exact were it taken as a general model of behavior. This construal of artistic expression is quite compatible with modernist formal values, for the marginality and cost of the effort speaks against its general emulation, and the reality the artwork presents is, in fact, anomalous to the ordinary representations of social order. In this context, even extreme forms of expression do not violate the autonomy of art, and the borders between art and non-art remain secured.

The themes of form and expression can both be traced back to historical sources for their justification. Form, given its Kantian origins in the purposiveness of natural beauty, can have no objectives short of the universality of its cognitive findings; and artistic intentions, within the characterization given by Schopenhauer, are only fulfilled when the artwork penetrates the secrets of the will and thereby bequeathes immortality to its maker. This second is of particular interest here: "Immortality," of course, is the ultimate counter to social affliction; it pits the individual against the social order and, despite all, ensures victory for the individual. In one sense, this also ensures the individual's autonomy, for immortality, whether historical or spiritual, negates all the suffered dependencies in a lived life. In another sense, however, the social order, through the promises of immortality, is relieved of the obligation to provide autonomy for a living life—this being the concern of a higher process. The move from the soul's immortality to the artist's version replaces transcendence with history. For Hegel, these come to the same thing, but even in the secular climate of early modernism, the concepts are analogous. The artistic expressions that merit intentional pursuit expand our sense of the world but would threaten that world were they to be accepted as our communal sense. In this, the efforts of saints and geniuses are alike. Kept within the realm of art, however, these expressions are safely distanced and take on the status of edifying fictions rather than models for imitation. Importantly, under this view, the expressivity in artworks is best understood as a reference to the nature of an exceptional individual rather than to the interests of any social group this individual might exemplify or be taken to represent.

In late modernism, as the appeal of, even the historical version of, immortality waned, the threat of antagonism between expression and social order was mollified in a different way: The solitary figure of genius was replaced by a broad communal preoccupation with the benefits of creativity, and artistic activity became codified through familiar forms and practices. As a consequence, the content of expression was made compatible with the consensual sensibilities of groups, while the social implications of that content remained sequestered within art.

The transition into postmodernism further lessens the disparity between high art and mass culture, but the weakening of this distinction also moves creativity closer to the heterogeneous sources of mass culture for its contents. Importantly, this constitutes a move away from the value of individual creativity and toward the expressive concerns of groups.

In early modernism, the source of intention is invariably private and difficult to reach or justify. This is the intentionality of the individual artist, and it is the more elusive, disturbing, and valuable as that solitary artist tends toward "genius." In postmodernism, the value of intention is retained, but now it functions as a demarcator of groups. It has a consensual source and its tracing is a matter of agreement, an affirmation of the beliefs and shared peculiarities that identify the group: black art, feminist art, gay art, minority ethnic—Hispanic, American Indian—art, art of the handicapped. The list stretches and changes with groups subdividing or coming together as interests coincide or diverge. These are the sorts of groups from which, hitherto, one "escaped" in order to become an artist, in order to find an identity in that world beyond one's parochial origins. In the modernist world, this achievement of a new identity, whether of a "bohemian" or "artist" or simply a "bon vivant," signified reaching a center—of the self and its existential meaning. It soon became evident, however, that the late modernist commodification of the modalities of self-expression generated a world full of escapees—with as many centers. In such a world, identity is threatened by the ubiquity of the images of individuation; and the defensive move, one that presages postmodernism, is to shift the quest for identity from the self to a group. Through this process, the pointlessness—now—of a solitary quest is transformed into the welcome urgency of a communal one. This is, in effect, a return to origins.

In his role as art critic of *The Nation,* Arthur Danto wrote a review of the visual arts section of the 1991 Spoleto Festival U.S.A. held in Charleston, South Carolina. This section, evidently quite at cross-purposes with the rest of the festival, consisted of site-specific works exhibited in various parts of town. The notion of site-specificity has political as well as aesthetic connotations, for it challenges the "neutrality" through which museums protect "disinterested" appreciation from nonaesthetic distractions. In the Spoleto exhibition, a number of artists turned this challenge into an overt correlation between the site, its social nexus, and the content of the artwork. I quote from a section of Danto's review: "*House of the Future* was the work of the legendary black artist David

Hammons, who chose a site in a black neighborhood rarely touched by the Spoleto festivities. Its chief component is a sort of a model of the classic Charleston single house, only comically thin, about as wide as a doorway. It is deliberately unfinished, and on the side facing the street, the artist has written a message about the myths that African-Americans have accepted regarding their character. The work is intended to elevate the consciousness of the local youth, to teach them something about architecture, carpentry, themselves. And it may achieve these ends. But friends of mine visited a nearby church and discussed the house with some of the blacks, who were deeply fearful that *their* future was tied to such skinny houses, that maybe they were going to have to live in houses like that, and instead of hope, the alien presence of this building in their midst had awakened a sense of powerlessness and trepidation."[8]

As indicated by this review, the postmodern "return to origins" is not easy; for although the original departure now finds its best reasons in the return, the language learned while away must be reconciled with the original. This may only be a problem for a single, transitional, generation—or it may run deeper: the act of reconciling being the *point* of the art at issue.

The shift in postmodernism toward constituting the creative self within the intentionality of a group requires a revision in the notions not only of individual expression but also of the receptive sensibility. Here, an appreciation adequate to the new art is a communal practice, unexceptionally intertwined with many other practices. The singular, deeply anchored introspection that modernism demands of taste is no longer adequate, for it cannot adjust to the flexible pan-attentiveness demanded by postmodern art. Paradoxically, reasons for this change in appreciative venue can be found in some consequences of the success of modern art. The treasures pursued by solitary psychic excavation in the first half of the twentieth century became all too available on the communal surface in the second half. As with sacred relics, there came to be more certified artworks than could be attributed to the rare appearances of genius. The exclusivity of modernist individuation, appreciative and creative, was no longer supported by the populism that, perhaps unwittingly, a successful modernism generated.

Appreciation, in postmodernism, is not premised on acquisition. Collecting the artifacts of great art is now an investor's sport, one with antiquarian overtones, for speculative interest in "collectibles" does not extend much past modern art. The postwar rage to collect—that expiation of a prior parochial indifference to the radical art of early modernism—is now satisfied. Artists, by the same token, increasingly avoid correlating expression with the historical endurance of their works; and, as that ambition fades, the luxury of being misunderstood in the present also passes. Postmodern artworks take on the familiarity of advertising copy and, like such copy, vie with each other for immediate attention. In this context, the advanced artist is one who satisfies intentionality in the presentation of the work. This cannot occur unless the work is politicized, unless it bypasses formalist aloofness and becomes a demand that needs to be *confronted* rather than merely appreciated. Consider, for example, a work of Jenny Holzer called *Times Square Spectacolor Board, 1982.* This large illuminated work is perched on a building facing that famous intersection, and it confronts all who happen to look with the message: ABUSE OF POWER COMES AS NO SURPRISE.

Artworks that confront, even as artifacts, are essentially actions and, as such, do not—need not—survive the consequence of these actions. It is in this sense that they are not collectibles. Postmodern works are transient things: handouts, performance pieces, installations, disposables; they are messages, allusions, exhortations, admonitions, and, thus, have the incidental artifactuality of language. To ask formal beauty of them is suspect, for it has a proclivity to cloud the issue at hand. Also suspect is the individual who seeks to reclaim the work's expression by separating it from its social situation, for such a one is often (politically) untrustworthy.

Creativity, in this context of action, finds its immortality in the reception of the artwork's present demands, whether these are satisfied or not. Demands, in order to be met, must be clearly presented; and unmet demands, the next time around, must be differently—if not more clearly—presented. Such are the postmodern imperatives of style. Appreciation, here, requires a willingness to engage these actions, a willingness brought on, in part, by understanding that, like it or not, we are all part of the work at hand, and that indifference to its demands is the new parochialism.

Postmodernism as Criticism The critical role of modern art is directed at the "illusions" of modern society—those sophistries of rhetoric and signification that are imposed on the naive by the predatory as a defense against progress. The modernist faith in its own success is based upon the unswerving belief that direction produces method, which, in turn, is based on the Hegelian notion of progressive identity of event and account—that everything conceived as joined is joined, and that everything, in good time, will be.[9] Criticism, as the ideological extension of progress is, therefore, veridical and univocal in principle; taken practically, it is a reliable guide to the future. In this teleological context, the message has both logical and practical priority over its medium, and its vehicle—for our purposes here, artists and their works—is a contingent, replaceable means. Nevertheless, given that univocity prefers clarity, a limitation on messengers is desirable, and thus, we have the modernist limit of the avant-garde. The avant-garde functions as a prescriptive elite that presents significations of the future to an audience that fears the portents less than the consequences of disbelief. The conjunction of belief and elitism is essential, for otherwise, the avant-garde would dissolve—worse, expand—into squabbling interest groups. My contention is that in the ideologically skeptical climate of late modernism, this is precisely what happened.

Modernism begins with its attack on the ideologies of academic art; it ends with its being attacked by the ideologies of popular art. Both attacks are successful. To the early modern sensibility, academic art is an art of excess: Formal autonomy is stymied by obligatory reference to the trappings of fashion and manners, and artistic autonomy is undermined by the demands of professional service. The critical razor of modernism transfers these academic obligations from "fine" art to other, "popular" media, thus reserving for itself an art whose attenuation increases its potency in the symbolization of progress.

Given this scenario, the incursions of popular art into postmodernism can be seen as a new accommodation to the needs of a society that has rejected the ideal of progress and is now experiencing a present without a direction. One consequence of this accommodation is the demotion of autonomy from an artistic ideal to a specific kind of image—one of many in the crowded lexicon of newly reputable images. The look and sound of autonomy has now become a familiar style among styles, and alert artists find little threat to *their* autonomy in the polyvocity of these new images. In this chronicle, there is a circle of sorts between beginnings and ends. The end of modernism is a return to that subordination of art by social practice from which it was rescued by the ideal of progress. But this, of course, reveals the Janus face of the Hegelian legacy: the historical achievement of artistic autonomy that a later, higher stage renders irrelevant.

In postmodernism, there is no higher, only later, and hence, no ideal of progress, only a spectrum of achievable expectations. Consequently, there are no atavistic illusions to be sought out and shattered by a radical rationality; there is no academy and no avant-garde. Competitors in the arts find the rewards of "historical immortality" too ephemeral an ideal, even something of a hoax; and they regard "historical inevitability" in much the same way—although some still appeal to it as a matter of marketing strategy.

All this does not mean, however, that the history of postmodernism begins with the denial that there is anything to be attacked in the past or anything to be projected into the future. Modernism erred when it taught us that "purpose" can only be teleologically inspired. The ideological task in postmodernism, then, is to authenticate reasons for art making that are not trivial or empty, but that do not appeal to the special predictive "force" in artworks.[10] The new question for art theory is how to interweave concepts of social and aesthetic value without imputing historical necessity to the preferred patterns.

In his book on the German artist Anselm Kiefer, *Fire on the Earth,* John Gilmour quotes and comments on a conversation between Kiefer and the artist-theoretician Joseph Beuys. As this bears directly on the question of postmodernism and history, I excerpt it here: " '*Beuys:* . . . No god can help us anymore; we have to become gods ourselves. *Kiefer:* Thats a completely linear way of looking at things, with a beginning and a goal. *Beuys:* There's always a beginning and an end. *Kiefer:* But I always see more circular movements and the simultaneity of everything.' Thus, Kiefer's view places him outside the artistic vanguard, who want to be the visionaries who usher in future history. In Beuys's case, that means moving toward the era when every person would be an artist."[11]

These viewpoints are both rejections of the notion of history as progress. Beuys's vision is strangely like the Rousseauian one of autonomous individuals whose creativities minimally intersect in an ample and nonoppressive space. Kiefer's is more a Nietzschean return to the tribal collectivity of bodily functions, earth, and myth. Beuys is close to the present American experience of a sectarian, polyvocal, eclectic postmodernism, while Kiefer offers intimations of a European resurgence of ancient memories and suppressed allegiances.

The postmodernism I describe here is also one that is based on the concept of a socially pervasive creativity, but its artworks are directed at present goals. Because of its responsiveness to immediate events, such art is vulnerable to the charge that it is empty and trivial. This charge seems symptomatic of a nostalgia for the ideal of progress, the concern that today's art does not, in some important sense, "transcend" the concerns of its own society. Against this, it can be argued that arts that are instrumentally concerned with achieving the social objectives of specific groups have no reason to transcend these objectives, especially for the sake of another set of general ideals. "Artistic transcendence," in this view, is part of the history of modernism—with its baggage of Eurocentrism, paternalism, idealism, et cetera—and its denial strengthens the hope that this history can be rectified or even rewritten. It is in this sense that aesthetic and political processes come together in postmodern art. With "inevitability" no longer a helpmate, art seeks a dimension of public familiarity that is, at least, compatible with the scope necessary for political influence. Here, the metholo-gies of the popular arts show their strength.

It is worth noting that the radical forms of modern art, which originate in critical opposition to cultivated taste, later become the standards of that taste, while postmodernism, employing the familiar forms and techniques of the popular arts, criticizes modern taste for its recent collusion with the continuing patterns of social inequity. This collusion is often identified with the center-left political doctrine of "gradualism," and this, in turn, is associated with institutionalized modernism. These institutions—museums, academic departments, endowments—are now ideologically vulnerable to critical attack from a spectrum of extreme positions and have become defensive against pressures to alter their tempo of change. In this sense, postmodern art is not an attack on "tradition"; rather, it is an an attack on that political gradualism whose championing of modern art helped it become the dominant art of the century. The modernist insistence on the disengagement of art from *specific* action in the social sphere, in favor of the formalized support of a *tendency* in social change, effectively reduces the uses of art in present interests of disaffected groups. Through this disengagement, modern art becomes the model of centrist values. The tendencies toward abstraction and reduction, once powerful as evocations of ideality and essence, and, thereby, of "progress," now identify symbols of established power.

Against this postmodern version of "criticism," modernism can point to its institutions as a sign of its (historical) success, and it can deny that political motives are to be read into the effort to cultivate good taste and artistic excellence. Yet, the battle seems joined: The claim that art, to be "fine," must transcend its parochial origins denigrates those works that claim to represent the interests of those origins. The postmodern argument, as I represent it here, is that depoliticization is itself a political stance that is supported by the flawed notion that art is incidentally political and essentially art. The challenge that postmodern works level at this ideology is not only through their confrontational content, but through their function as performatives of, and for, these various contents.

The artist Eva Hesse, whose tragically short career ended in 1970, developed a body of work that, although very much part of the American vanguard, also anticipated concerns I attribute here to postmodernism. She considered her work as a three-dimensional furthering of the Pollock tradition, in that it continued the emphasis on process and resistance to closure.[12] Yet, as in the work *Right After, 1969,* she introduced materials—latex, string, gauze netting—that are soft, difficult to relocate, and impermanent. The implication is this: Such works are site specific; they resist commodification; and they evoke materials and sensibilities historically associated with women. While Hesse did not take these characteristics to be central to her art, she took them to be lived experiences that she did not separate from her art. Lucy Lippard, in her book on Hesse, writes on this point: "Women are always derogatorily associated with crafts, and have been conditioned towards such chores as tying, sewing, knotting, wrapping, binding, knitting, and so on. Hesse's art transcends the cliche of 'detail as women's work' while at the same time incorporating these notions of ritual as antidote to isolation and despair."[13]

In regard to the familiar admonition that there is no women's art or black art or gay art, et cetera, there is only good and bad art, the now familiar rejoinder is that if women's art, for example, must be good as art before it is good as women's art, then that art is judged by standards that are part of the problem a "women's art" art seeks to address. This rejoinder implies that value judgments about artworks (must) include their capacities in projecting the values of their (social) origins: Women's art has value in the context of women's interests, which include the effectiveness of that art in presenting these interests to the political majority. And the transference of aesthetic value to these origins is justified by reference to histories of exploitation. In this way, the question about maintaining value in the absence of teleology is answered. Belief in the function of art as criticism is maintained, even as the belief in art as a (transcendental) symbol of progress is discarded.

5. QUESTIONS FOR THE FUTURE

The vesting of small groups with the theoretical paraphernalia—ontic, normative, affective—once sustained by an autonomous and unified art poses considerable problems. For one, each such group must remain satisfied with the limits imposed by its specialized ideology. This is not easy: Covert longings for a universalizing value, the temptation to return to a centralized art world—these must be scrupulously guarded against. Another problem has to do with the cohesiveness of the group: If the primary orientation is sexual, then secondary political preferences may conflict; if political, then sexual conflicts may arise; if racial or ethnic, then agreement about principles may be weakened by identity differences; and so forth. Breakdowns in cohesiveness, of course, diminish political effectiveness. When conflicts arise, group members face the conflicting choices of forming still smaller units or, in exasperation, of giving up on collective identity and returning to a previous self of artist-as-individual. In the latter case, a unified art world, however illusory, offers a familiar haven.

In recent years, there has been considerable acrimony in

the United States between, on the one hand, groups and ideologies I describe here as postmodern and, on the other, governmental policies on the arts and public imagery.[14] As these policies are being tested by a number of confrontational works, there is increasing debate over the ethics of placing limitations on artistic practices and, in general, over the role of government in the arts. The focus at present is on images of sexual "deviancy" and the "misuse" of national and religious symbols. At issue is not only the purported assault these images make on collective beliefs and sensibilities, but the fact that a number of such exhibitions, and the artists involved, have received government funding. The faction that favors placing limitations on these practices begins with the demand that public support for such activities be eliminated, and continues with the demand for a general policy of censorship in the arts and public media. As the works involved in this dispute have been variously labeled "pornographic," "treasonous," and "blasphemous," one sees in this demand an enlargement and consolidation of the target through the association of negativities—sexual, political, religious—each type of work being tainted with the sins of the others. Paradoxically, through this premise of collective guilt, the works in question come again to symbolize a kind of unified art—a new avant-garde—whether their authors want the common association or not.

Another side of this picture is the defense put up against this threat of censorship by those institutions, including government agencies, that fund, exhibit, and distribute the works in question. This defense seeks to maintain a position of control through selective compromise: The aim is to continue as a benevolent influence on the creation and projection of such works while, at the same time, accepting the necessary imposition, the inevitability, of some controls.[15] The stance of "gradualism" is much in evidence here.

The policy of governmental support of the arts, as I believe, is itself a form of political gradualism, for it is a way of maintaining the ideology of a unified and autonomous art, essentially a modernist ideology, by selectively underwriting the efforts of disaffected groups. The notion of "unity" is maintained by identifying these diverse efforts as all developments, however attenuated, out of the modernist avant-garde. Through this explanation, the political ramifications of the more confrontational works are both protected and neutralized by the emphasis on the primacy of their aesthetic qualities. Thus, the modernist thesis of "aesthetic autonomy" is given a new social identity.

However, this institutional defense, notwithstanding its past history, is not guaranteed present success. For those groups directly antagonized by this art, groups with little interest in the art world or in the social value of aesthetic privilege, the works in question are seen as direct assaults on the ideological base of their own political power. Strangely, this confrontation has the virtue of exteriorizing the political issues, the conflicts between group interests, that are at stake. These issues seem not to be of the kind that can be resolved by institutional fiat—by having a solitary, misunderstood genius whisked away into aesthetic custody. The contest provoked by postmodernism is *between* aesthetic and political autonomy—the freedom of art against the freedom to protest. On the one side, the freedom of art can be assured, and support for it continued, by having it relinquish those characteristics that, it could be said, "have never been" part of art-as-art. This argues for the re-aestheticizing of art, and the wanted version is an art that embraces "progress" while discarding "criticism." This is the institutional contender for the mantle of postmodernism.

As to the other side: The choice of art's political autonomy, the freedom to protest, entails the evident loss of opportunities for artistic performance, exhibition, and publication. Such a loss is unwelcome but not unfamiliar; it is in fact a romantic staple of the "old" avant-garde. There is something of greater importance, however: Making this choice involves the metaphysical gamble of having misconstrued art, of having gone beyond its limits in the (perhaps, naive) belief that its limits will follow along, as they have in the past. The fear of losing this gamble is Hegelian teleology resurrected as the specter of having missed out on the historical mainstream. Taking the gamble wagers that there no longer is a mainstream—that there is no cogent reason why artworks should still vie for privileged roles in a historical narrative that has lost its way and its point. Here, a skeptic might say that any artwork that rests its future on such a view will assuredly have little to contribute to *the* historical narrative. But the rejoinder to this, one that would authenticate postmodernism, is that such a view contains the only good reasons for continuing to make art.

NOTES AND INDEX

Notes

CHAPTER ONE

1. Immanuel Kant, *Critique of Judgment*, tr. J. H. Bernard (New York: Hafner Press, 1951). Cited as *CJ* hereafter.

2. Immanuel Kant, *Critique of Pure Reason*, tr. Norman Kemp Smith (New York: St. Martin's Press, 1965). Cited as *CPR* hereafter.

3. Immanuel Kant, *Critique of Practical Reason*, tr. Lewis White Beck, (New York: Bobbs-Merrill, 1956). Cited as *CPrR* hereafter.

4. Kant, *CJ*, 12.

5. For empirical judgments, the Kantian categories begin with "quantity," followed by "quality." In the judgment of beauty this order is reversed. As reflection on beauty provides the particular "for which the universal has to be found" (*CJ*, 15), the starting point is the immediate one of sensation—of its quality.

6. See Hans Vaihinger, *Philosophy of "As-If,"* tr. C. K. Ogden, 6th ed. (London: Routledge and Kegan Paul, 1949).

7. Kant, "Transcendental Analytic," ch. 3 in *CPR*, 257–75.

8. Kant, "Dialectic of Pure Practical Reason," ch. 2 in *CPrR*, 147–53.

9. Kant, "Dialectic of the Aesthetical Judgment," in *CJ*, 183–87.

10. Kant defines taste as "the faculty for judging a priori of the communicability of feelings that are bound up with a given representation (without the mediation of a concept)" (*CJ*, 138). This can also serve as his definition of appreciation. The first book is devoted to an analysis of the "moments" of the judgment of taste.

11. In the "Analytic of the Sublime" (in *CJ*, 82–181) Kant does not specifically correlate "sublimity" and "genius." He begins the section with an analysis of the mathematical and

dynamical sublime, and then somewhat ambiguously sandwiches the discussion of artistic creativity and works of art between sections on the deduction and dialectic of aesthetic judgment. But the metaphors Kant uses to characterize sublimity he also uses in his account of genius. Kant's analysis of the "faculties" that comprise genius contrasts the pair "imagination-spirit" with the pair "understanding-taste." I interpret the former as the "creative" pair, which can be described through the characteristics of the natural sublime: power, magnitude, nonsubsumption under rules. Kant imports the latter pair from his account of appreciation and uses it to temper the extravagances of genius with the discipline that "clips its wings . . . but, at the same time, gives guidance as to where and how far it may extend itself if it is to remain purposive" (*CJ*, 163) Here, Kant is concerned with balancing the freedom of genius with the intelligibility—the accessibility to judgment—required of the artwork. This is an Enlightenment balance that is later skewed toward the freedom of artistic expression. To my mind, it is the Kantian transfer of sublimity from nature to art (via genius) that establishes a basis for the later Romantic association of artistic creativity, rather than rationality, with nature. This eventuates, in my tracing, with the modernist linkage between creativity and the sublimities of the psyche—between creativity and "inner nature."

12. *Ibid.* Kant's move to limit the relation between reflective judgment and the concept of deity is most extensively discussed in the "Critique of Teleological Judgment," in *CJ*, 312–27.

13. Kant calls natural beauty "free"—as opposed to "dependent"—beauty (*CJ*, 65–66) and elucidates this with many examples throughout the work, e.g., on pages 41, 80, 145, 193.

14. The Greeks locate their images of the unity of design and freedom in the human figure and in architecture. In the late eighteenth and nineteenth centuries, this unity is found in the landscape that presents us with the image of "purposiveness without purpose," Kant's third requirement for aesthetic judgment. It is interesting to note how much Kant relies on visual images in his argument.

15. Kant, *CJ*, 145.

16. *Ibid.*, "Analytic of the Sublime," secs. 51–53.

17. *Ibid.*, 164–66.

18. *Ibid.*, 166–68.

19. *Ibid.*, 169–74.
20. *Ibid.*, 142.
21. *Ibid.*, 150.
22. *Ibid.* The second part of the discussion on "Aesthetical Judgment" is devoted to the sublime. Section 29 of this part compares the bases for judgments of beauty and sublimity, referring the first to "understanding," the second to "reason." Kant also makes a distinction between the mathematical and dynamical sublime. While this is important for his overall thesis, it is the dynamical version that has immediate aesthetic application.
23. *Ibid.*, "General Remark," 77, 78.
24. *Ibid.*, 109.
25. *Ibid.*, 108.
26. This correlation between sublimity and morality as an "infinite task" comes out of conversations with my late colleague, Steven Schwarzschild.
27. See Plato, *Ion.*

CHAPTER TWO

1. Arthur Schopenhauer, *The World as Will and Representation*, 2 vols., tr. E. F. J. Payne (New York: Dover, 1969). Cited as *WWR* hereafter. The first volume of this work, originally published in 1819, is divided into four books: Books one and two contain the account of Schopenhauer's two metaphysical principles, representation and will; book three presents the aesthetic theory; and book four the ethics. Volume two, written some twenty-five years later, is divided into four supplements, and is a commentary and elaboration of the material in the first volume.
2. As with Kant and Hegel, the value of art for Schopenhauer lies primarily in its epistemic function. But he alone holds that art functions to encourage us to choose the contemplative life—the only adequate moral response to his metaphysical first principle: the noumenal will.
3. The "principle of sufficient reason" is developed in an earlier work (1813) of the same name. The philosophical importance of Indian philosophy, e.g., the Upanishads and the Vedas, is developed in part four of *WWR*, but references to this are found throughout the work.

4. To the extent that Schopenhauer admits gradations of the will's manifestations in nature, he accepts, if not "progress," at least an increasing complexity in nature's temporal course. The human capacity for symbolic behavior marks the highest level of complexity. Yet, this is not a telic account in that the process leads nowhere—there is no God, and no reunion. Human wisdom lies in this realization and the concommitant rejection of the will's imperatives to action.

5. See Immanuel Kant, "Critique of the Teleological Judgment," in *Critique of Judgment,* tr. J. H. Bernard (New York: Hafner Press, 1951), 205–339.

6. Kant uses the sublime to redirect mind to the satisfactions inherent in its own rational capacities. In contrast, Romantic art extends mind into an identification with sublimity in nature. This also heralds a new identification of mind with body, will with sensibility—at the expense of the dispassionate stance that Kant requires for judgment. Later, Expressionist art relocates nature entirely within the self, through images of the subconscious, thus giving the joining of mind and nature a new locus.

7. See Theodor Adorno, "World Spirit and Natural History," in *Negative Dialectics,* tr. E. B. Ashton (New York: Continuum Press, 1973), 300–360.

8. Here, the Kantian emphasis on beauty in nature contrasts with Schopenhauer's emphasis on art. For Kant, nature provides us with beauty through a special form of appearance. Schopenhauer finds beauty in the images of things beyond appearances—in the "forms"—that art provides. The consequences for morality are also quite different: for Kant, an encouragement to engage the world; for Schopenhauer, withdrawal.

9. Schopenhauer, *WWR* 1:201–4.

10. *Ibid.* See part four.

11. The construal of sublimity as a model for the autonomous, antisocial individual, is one of Schopenhauer's bequests to Nietzsche. See Nietzsche's *Beyond Good and Evil.*

12. Schopenhauer, *WWR,* 1:179. Plato's theory of "Forms" is developed in a number of his dialogues, perhaps most extensively in the *Phaedo* and the *Republic.*

13. See Plato's *Republic,* books II and X.

14. Schopenhauer, *WWR* 1:185.

15. *Ibid.,* 191.

16. Ibid. 2:612. It has been suggested that interpreting Schopenhauer as a Stoic can lead to an ethic of accommodation—a Hobbesian "materialism" within which the ideologies that rationalize willed ambition are discounted, but the opportunities that promote comfort and well-being are taken. But this interpretation minimizes Schopenhauer's fascination with the very different accommodations of passivity and withdrawal that characterize Indian and Christian mysticism (See 573–88, and 613–33). One should also take into account the appeal of Schopenhauer's writings for the social marginals—bohemians, beatniks, flower-children—of later periods.

17. Ibid. 1:255. Discussion of the "classification of the arts" is found in section 52.

18. Ibid., 263–64.

19. Suzanne Langer presents an aesthetic theory that has many similarities to Schopenhauer's. See her *Philosophy in a New Key* (Cambridge, Mass.: Harvard University Press, 1942) and *Feeling and Form* (New York: Charles Scribner's Sons, 1953). For a critique of her theory, one that could also be applied to Schopenhauer, see Samuel Bufford, "Langer Evaluated: Suzanne Langer's Two Philosophies of Art," in *Aesthetics*, ed. George Dickie and R. J. Sclafani (New York: St. Martin's Press, 1977), 166–82.

20. See Descartes, *Third Meditation.*

CHAPTER THREE

1. Both Kant and Schopenhauer theorize within a dualistic framework, through such categorical distinctions as between knowledge and the world, between forms of knowing, and between appearance and reality. For Hegel, such distinctions are provisional and progressively expendable in the evolution of thought; thus, his system resists categorical parsing.

2. G.W.F. Hegel, "Absolute Knowing," in *Phenomenology of Spirit*, tr. A. V. Miller (Oxford: Oxford University Press, 1977), ch. 8, 479–93. The German term *Geist* has been translated as both "mind" and "spirit." I prefer "spirit" (and use it throughout this work) because "mind" is overly directed to cognition and is thus misleading for aesthetic theory.

3. The Hegelian term *aufheben* captures the double sense of "transcending" and "retaining." This sense characterizes the dialectical process.

4. Hegel, introduction to *Phenomenology*, 46–57.

5. See Quentin Lauer, *A Reading of Hegel's Phenomenology of Spirit* (New York: Fordham University Press, 1976) and William Desmond, *Art and the Absolute* (New York: State University of New York Press, 1986).

6. Hegel, "Absolute Knowing," in *Phenomenology*, 479–93.

7. See Hegel, *Reason in History*.

8. See Kant, *On History*.

9. G. W. F. Hegel, *Aesthetics*, tr. T. M. Knox (Oxford: Oxford University Press, 1975), 1:2. This translation presents the *Aesthetics* in two volumes: The first volume contains the introduction, part 1 on the Idea (Ideal) of artistic beauty, and part 2 on the development of the Ideal into the particular forms of art. The second volume comprises part 3, which presents Hegel's system of the individual arts.

10. Arthur Schopenhauer, *The World as Will and Representation*, tr. E.F.J. Payne, (New York: Dover 1969), 1:179–81.

11. Hegel, *Aesthetics* 1:143–74.

12. See Jean Hyppolite, *Genesis and Structure of Hegel's Phenomenology of Spirit*, tr. Samuel Cherniak and John Heckman (Evanston, Ill.: Northwestern University Press, 1974), 51–59.

13. Hegel, *Aesthetics* 1:299–377.

14. *Ibid.*, 311.

15. *Ibid.*, 476–501.

16. *Ibid.*, 517–72.

17. *Ibid.*, 364.

18. *Ibid.*, 538.

19. *Ibid.* 2:889.

20. *Ibid.*, 903.

21. *Ibid.*, 951–55.

22. *Ibid.*, 960.

23. *Ibid.*, 960.

24. See Karl Popper, *The Poverty of Historicism* (New York: Harper and Row, 1957).

25. See Hegel, *Reason in History*, ch.1.

26. See Arthur Danto, *Narration and Knowledge* (New York: Columbia University Press, 1985).

27. Hegel, *Aesthetics* 1:602–11.

CHAPTER FOUR

1. Immanuel Kant, *Critique of Judgment,* tr. J.H. Bernard (New York: Hafner Press, 1951), 39. Cited as *CJ* hereafter.

2. *Ibid,* 37.

3. Kant equates appreciation with a universal pleasure that is commendable to all only if it is not relativized by personal preferences. Taste that judges accordingly is "good"; lesser varieties cannot sustain universality.

4. Kant, *Metaphysics of Morals,* (New York: Library of Liberal Arts, 1990), 14.

5. Kant, *CJ,* 149.

6. *Ibid,* 80.

7. *Ibid,* "Critique of the Teleological Judgment."

8. In some early popular essays, Kant outlines his views on the nature of history and social progress. These amount to demonstrations of teleological judgment's application to particular issues. The most pertinent essays are "Idea for a Universal History from a Cosmopolitan Point of View" and "An Old Question Raised Again: Is the Human Race Constantly Progressing?" (Both essays can be found in Kant, *On History,* ed. L. W. Beck. [New York: Library of Liberal Arts, 1963].)

9. I discuss this in my *Art and Concept,* (Amherst: University of Massachusetts Press, 1987), 33–34.

10. Kant, *CJ,* 150–51.

11. *Ibid.,* 163–64.

12. The notion "candidate for appreciation" has its origins in the work of George Dickie.

CHAPTER FIVE

1. Arthur Schopenhauer, *The World as Will and Representation,* tr. E.F.J. Payne (New York: Dover 1969), 2:407. Cited as *WWR* hereafter.

2. Aesthetic "necessity" and "universality" are, for Kant, based upon an "ought." Yet, as Schopenhauer complains about the similarly grounded categorical imperative, it "leaps into the world . . . in order to command there." In this sense, taste moves from the theoretical function Kant assigns it to become an instrument for social constancy in manners and art. See "Criticism of the Kantian Philosophy," in *WWR,* 1:523.

3. Schopenhauer, *WWR* 1:212–67. In his categories of art, Schopenhauer moves from natural to cultural, objective to subjective, and thereby offers a division that has, at least, structural resemblances to Hegel's. Schopenhauer's informal schema antedates Hegel's more extensive and formal categorization by some fifteen years, and their efforts differ in important respects—particularly in the value placed on historical process. Hegel nowhere, to my knowledge, indicates any interest in Schopenhauer's work.

4. *Ibid.*, 392.

5. The transition, here from the neoclassic to the romantic artist, can be followed in a further evolution—into the "avant-garde" artist of twentieth-century modernism.

6. As I indicate in the first section of this chapter, Schopenhauer gives the capacity for "containing truth" to both art and philosophy. The former does so "virtually and implicitly," and the latter "actually and explicitly." *WWR* 2:407.

7. *WWR* 1:190.

8. *Ibid*, 267.

9. Plato, *Republic*, book X.

10. *WWR* 1:267.

CHAPTER SIX

1. The more encompassing the scope of a philosophical system, the more variegated its concept of truth is likely to be. Hegel is perhaps the prime example: He posits an overarching "truth" that is then variously distributed among the historical positions and conceptual tasks of his various symbolic forms. Truth is associated more with novelty, suggestiveness, and scope than with verification. As his dialectical method is inherently unstable, no methodology is fixed and no medium excluded for the presentation of truth—not even the arts. The later delimiting of truth to its logical and empirical forms may well have signaled the end of idealist metaphysics; correspondingly, the indifference to truth in art may have been a factor in the (still later) decline of modernism.

2. G.W.F. Hegel, *Reason in History*, tr. Robert S. Hartman (New York: Bobbs-Merrill, 1953), sec. 3, 67.

3. Nelson Goodman does much to relieve art of the noncognitive status given it by analytic philosophy. His thesis that visual

works, e.g., show particular patterns of compliance with characteristics that identify all symbolic forms, aesthetic and nonaesthetic, returns some cognitive function to art. See his *Languages of Art* (Indianapolis, Ind.: Bobbs-Merrill, 1968). Also, his suggestion that the "actual" world is composed of many worlds blunts the force of the "fact-fiction" dichotomy. See his *Ways of Worldmaking* (Indianapolis, Ind.: Hackett, 1978).

4. See Hegel's *Science of Logic,* tr. W. H. Johnston and L. G. Struthers (New York: Macmillan, 1929), especially vol. 1, book 2, "Contradiction," 58–70.

5. It is important to note that, for Hegel, art ends when its form of truth becomes inadequate to the kinds of distinctions reason is capable of, not when it has been "found out" never to have been a truth-bearing symbol—as a noncognitivist might claim (see Chapter Nine).

6. Hegel, *Aesthetics,* tr. T. M. Knox (Oxford: Oxford University Press, 1975), 1:11.

7. *Ibid.,* 111.

8. *Ibid.,* 535.

9. See Hegel, "The State," in *Reason in History,* (New York: Library of Liberal Arts, 1953), 49–67.

10. Hegel, *Aesthetics,* 2:947–48.

11. *Ibid.,* 899.

12. *Ibid.,* 887. Given Hegel's fascination with Napoleon, it seems particularly strange that he makes no reference to the French visual arts of his time, which, in the hands of Ingres, Delacroix, and Gericault, celebrated the emperor with extensive apotheoses.

13. *Ibid.,* 1110, 1131–32, 1156.

14. Hegel, *Reason in History,* 69.

15. Hegel, "The Truth of Self-certainty," in *Phenomenology of Spirit,* tr. A.V. Miller (Oxford: Oxford University Press, 1977) ch. 4. The relevant distinction is between "consciousness" and "self-consciousness," and the point at issue is the freedom of determination entailed in the latter stage. Hegel conjoins "progress" with "freedom" and, thus, in a nonmechanistic context does not take history to be predictable. Of course, he does take spirit's ascendency to be inevitable—but knowledge of this is retrospective.

16. Here can be cited Kandinsky's and Klee's interests in analogues between visual and musical form, also the many

variants of conceptual art that have roots in Duchamp, the "work-text" and "author-critic" elisions of New Criticism, etc.

17. The alliance between radical art and radical sociology is found in the Critical Theorists, e.g., Adorno, Benjamin, Horkheimer. It is also found, although more circumspectly, in the documents of the Bauhaus and, as well, in the writings of Mondrian and the Constructivists.

CHAPTER SEVEN

1. Cézanne, "Letter to Emil Bernard" 1904, in *Theories of Modern Art,* ed. Hershel Chipp, (Berkeley and Los Angeles: University of California Press, 1970), 19.

2. Modernist polemics have often characterized cubism as a style of transition—a dispenser of new structural ideas—to other styles with more radical and consequential programs. In retrospect, cubism, particularly the "analytic" phase, seems more like modernism's center.

3. See the comparison I draw between Mondrian and Kandinsky in my book *Art and Concept,* (Amherst: University of Massachusetts Press, 1987), ch. 1.

4. Clive Bell, "Art as Significant Form," in *Aesthetics,* ed. George Dickie and R. J. Sclafani (New York: St. Martin's Press, 1977), 36–48.

5. See David Hume, *Enquiry Concerning Human Understanding,* sec. 12. The correlation of the "competent judge" with the capacity for discerning the artistically beautiful can be traced back to Plato. See *Laws,* book II.

6. See Kant's preface to *Prolegomena to Any Future Metaphysics.*

7. Bell, "Art," 74.

8. *Ibid.*, 82.

9. Nietzsche claims the view from the pinnacle in which all conventionally based normative systematizations, such as Hume's, are exposed for their complicity against the autonomous individual. See his *Also Sprach Zarathustra.* This view becomes a standard of early modernism. But in late modernism, as I argue, the practice of autonomy itself becomes conventionalized.

10. For the received formalist thesis—that intention is neither necessary nor retrievable in interpretation—see W. K. Wimsatt, Jr., and Monroe Beardsley, "The Intentional Fallacy." in *The Verbal I Can*, ed. W. K. Wimsatt, Jr. (Lexington: University of Kentucky Press, 1954), ch. 1. This thesis has many recent counters: See E. D. Hirsch Jr., *Validity in Interpretation*, (New Haven, Conn.: Yale University Press, 1967), and Richard Wollheim *Painting as an Art* (Princeton, N.J.: Princeton University Press, 1987).

11. The shift in origins from "nature" to "self" parallels the historical move from pre-World War II European Expressionism (Soutine, Kokoshka) to the abstract Expressionism of post-war America (Pollock, de Kooning, Kline). Kandinsky's early abstractions are pivotal here. A frequently used metaphor for this shift from representational origins is the term "inscape."

12. "Becoming as one with nature" identifies the Dionysian pole of Nietzsche's aesthetic, in which fecundity is achieved at the expense of individual identity. The various "immolations" in Wagner's music dramas can be taken as symbolic of this union. See Nietzsche, *The Birth of Tragedy*.

13. The other Nietzschean aesthetic polarity is the Apollonian, wherein the realization of self through dream and fantasy is achieved at the expense of contact with the world of others. Freud removes the artist from the psychotic extreme of this polarity through the reality structures that the creation of art requires. See Sigmund Freud, "The Poet and Daydreaming," in *Collected Papers*, vol. 4 (London: Hogarth Press, 1934).

14. See "Surrealism and Painting" by André Breton, in *Theories of Modern Art*, ed. Herschel B. Chipp (Berkeley and Los Angeles: University of California Press, 1970), 402–9. Similarities between recurrences of theme and image in dream analysis and in artistic works were reified by Carl Jung through a psychoanalytic theory of the "collective unconscious." Here, such similarities become instantiations of the "universal archetypes" that comprise this realm. See Carl Jung, *Symbols of Transformation*, tr. R.F.C. Hull (Princeton, N.J.: Princeton University Press, 1956).

15. Sidney Janis, one of the earliest New York art dealers to show the new American art, documents this intersection between styles in his book, *Abstract and Surrealist Art in America*, (New York: William Bradford Press, 1944).

16. Leo Tolstoi, "What Is Art," in *Tolstoi On Art*, tr. Aylmer Maude (Boston: Small, Maynard & Co., 1924).

17. The relation between artistic autonomy and art's critical imperative is a major theme in the writings of the Critical Theorists: Adorno, Benjamin, Horkheimer, etc. In his excellent book, *Theory of the Avant-Garde* (Minneapolis: University of Minnesota Press, 1984), Peter Burger sees late modernism as "institutionalizing the avant-garde as art" (ch. 4). These writings have a Marxist-idealist orientation that, given the present ideological climate, exerts little influence on American popular criticism. Yet they are prescient about such consequences of modernism as the "commodification" of art and the loss of history as a catalyst for art. My study, here, does not attempt a cultural critique, although I do identify the postmodern reaction to late modernism as a "politicization" of art. In this sense, I indicate a reemergence of art's critical role that would accord with some convictions of the Critical Theorists—if not with all their tastes.

18. Also prominent in the Suprematist group were the visionary architect Vladimir Tatlin and the painters El Lissitsky and Goncharova. The Constructivist ("Realistic") Manifesto of 1920, written by the sculptors Gabo and Pevsner, is a clear argument for a new artistic beginning from a basis of pure abstraction.

19. See *Malevich,* by Larisa Zhvadova, tr. Alexander Lieven (New York: Thames and Hudson, 1982).

20. Kant, Schopenhauer, and Hegel all take pains to distinguish genuine from false novelty in the aesthetic sphere—through much the same distinction as between freedom and license in the moral sphere.

21. The phrase "tradition of the new," I believe, originates with the critic Harold Rosenberg. See my discussion of "tradition classes" in *Art and Concept,* ch. 6.

22. Roland Barthes, *Image, Music, Text* (New York: Hill and Wang, 1977).

23. *Ibid.,* 143.

24. *Ibid.,* 145.

25. *Ibid.,* 146.

26. *Ibid.,* 148.

CHAPTER EIGHT

1. Institutional pressure on artists in present-day society occurs in a variety of ways. Perhaps the most pervasive is the equation of vocation with success. Increasingly, as in the past three decades, the obscure artist is the failed artist. Then there is the second vocation of many artists—teaching. Here the pressures are via institutional citizenship and peer judgments for reappointment. Also, particularly in performance and installation arts, artists have come to rely on grant funding (see Chapter Nine, last section).

2. See Hegel, *Reason in History*, 3–10.

3. The phrase "dogmatic turn" comes from Richard Rorty; some of the sentiments—if not the specifics—of my discussion do as well.

4. The epistemic value of Expressionist art can be compared with that of symbolist (or surrealist) art. The latter is actually closer to Schopenhauer, in that emphasis is on the revelatory power of the symbol. Expressionism transfers epistemic force to process, thus allying revelation with dynamics—first the will, then the artist.

5. See Kant, *Metaphysics of Morals*, sec. 1.

6. The increase, between 1950 and 1980, in art programs as part of the degree-granting curricula in colleges and universities is considerable. See Joe H. Prince, *The Arts at State Colleges and Universities* (Washington, D.C.: American Association of State Colleges and Universities, 1990).

7. See Theodore Adorno, *Aesthetic Theory*, London: Routledge and Kegan Paul, 1984), ch. 9, 6.

8. Hegel, Introduction to *Aesthetics;* also sec. 3, ch. 1, 1a.

CHAPTER NINE

1. The question here is what else artworks must be in order to be art. Some interesting answers are George Dickie's "candidates for appeciation" ("Defining Art," *American Philosophical Quarterly* 6 [1969]:253–56), Arthur Danto's "members of the artworld," ("The Artistic Enfranchisement of Real Objects: The Artworld," *Journal of Philosophy* 61 [1964]:571–84), and Joseph Margolis's "embodiments." (*Art and Philosophy* [Atlantic Highlands, N.J.: Humanities Press, 1981], chs. 1–5).

2. See Paul Oscar Kristeller, "The Modern System of the Arts," *Journal of the History of Ideas* 12 (1951): 469–527.

3. The "end of art" thesis has been given its fullest modern formulation by Arthur Danto. See *The Philosophical Disenfranchisement of Art,* (New York: Columbia University Press,

1986) ch. 5. In its Hegelian origins, the thesis presumes art's historical supplantation in the teleological process by more purely cognitive symbols. Danto views art's "end" more as the end of the hold this ideology has over art—with the result that there is now a cultural dispersal of style through a plurality of origins and uses. I interpret Danto as viewing this to be a positive development in both art and culture.

4. The "unity of art" thesis has its counterpart in such "unity of science" principles as (*a*) all scientific methodologies have a common theoretical basis; (*b*) all statements of the particular sciences can, in principle, be restated in the foundational language of physics; (*c*) a context-free logical basis for language can be identified upon which veridical descriptions of the world are constructed. See my "Aufbau and Bauhaus; a Cross-realm Comparison," *Journal of Aesthetics and Art Criticism* 50 (Summer 1992):3.

5. See E. D. Hirsch, Jr., *Cultural Literacy* (New York: Random House, 1988).

6. See Arthur Danto, *Transfiguration of the Commonplace* (Cambridge, Mass.: Harvard University Press, 1981), ch. 1.

7. Hermann Hesse's novel, *Magister Ludi,* envisions a dichotomized world in which the aesthetic half, divested of its practical counterpart, can do nothing more than produce endless variations on its cultural past under the direction of the "master of the game."

8. *The Nation,* July 29–August 5, 1991.

9. See Hegel, *Phenomenology of Spirit,* esp. C. [Free Concrete Mind] (BB), "Spirit."

10. It seems to me that the modernist location of a historically prescient "force" in style is quite analogous to the concept of force in causal relationships that Hume so effectively argues against. See Hume's *Enquiry concerning Human Understanding,* ch. 7.

11. John Gilmour, *Fire on Earth: Anselm Kiefer and the Postmodern World,* (Philadelphia: Temple University Press, 1990), 140–41.

12. Lucy Lippard, *Eva Hesse* (New York: New York University Press, 1976), 188–92.

13. *Ibid.,* 209.

14. In 1990, political attacks on exhibitions of works funded by the National Endowment for the Arts sparked debate on the

government use of censorship in the arts. The debate became more complex through the evocation of laws against "obscenity" and the "desecration" of national symbols. Works of Robert Mapplethorpe and Andres Serrano were particularly at issue.

15. As a condition for continued funding, all parties were asked to affirm that the works exhibited, etc., would avoid certain controversial subject matter. This agreement would purportedly serve to keep jurisdiction in funding in the hands of arts professionals. At this writing, the issues remain unresolved.

Index

Aesthetics: instrumentalist, 156–157; systematic role, 2–5
Aesthetic themes: development, 2–5, 135–137, 193; "expression" to "intention," 145–157; inversions in postmodernism, 188; "progress" to "criticism," 157–169, 191; sources and issues, 1–9; "taste" to "form," 137–145; transformations, 9–13, 160–161
Analytic philosophy, 2, 120
Appreciation, 7; in Kant, 23, 25, 92–94; in Hegel, 121; in Schopenhauer, 50–52, 113
Architecture, 29, 31, 61, 77, 84, 107
Aristotle, 206
Art: abstract, 77, 140, 142, 152; and society, 148, 181–182, 186; autonomy of, 15, 28, 137, 138, 141–142, 162, 190, 193, 197, 207, 213, 220; class of, 189–192; end of, 14, 15, 73, 123–125, 130, 139, 159, 186, 191–195, 203, 237–238; fine, 28; vs. popular, 197–199, 202–204, 213; government in, 219–221; history of, 127, 183; in postmodernism, 195–197, 213–214, 217–218; in Hegel, 70–71, 74–82, 118–120, 125–131, 191; in Kant, 27–32; in Schopenhauer, 52–56, 60–63, 106–109; in Plato, 53, 54; in Tolstoy, 154–157; non-art, 178, 189; novelty in, 163, 236; post-art, 191–195, 199; style in, 95–98, 175, 200, 204; system of, 189, 192, 196; taste in, 92–98; unity of, 15, 188, 193, 199, 238
Artist: and sublimity, 147; Apollonian, 150, 235; as neurotic, 42, 114–115, 182; Dionysian, 148, 235; immortality, 207, 214; in Hegel, 84–86; in Kant, 38, 39, 54, 57; in modernism, 181–182; in Plato, 53, 54; in postmodernism, 208–209, 236–237; in Schopenhauer, 42, 53–60, 111–114, 147; self-expression, 148, 149
Avant-garde, 13, 117, 144, 157, 162–163, 185, 200–201, 213, 219, 221, 236

Barthes, Roland: and modernism, 170–171; author-work-critic, 164–171; author as person, 165, 168; as scriptor, 166, 167; as critic, 167–169; reader-scriptor-text, 169; texts as readings and writings, 169; play, 169
Bauhaus, 31
Beauty: and taste, 90, 92–98; appreciation of, 1, 7; in Hegel, 70, 71, 124, 128–129; in Kant, 23–27, 35–37, 63, 78, 226; in Schopenhauer, 47–52, 228
Beaux-arts, 31
Beethoven, Ludwig van, 126

Bell, Clive, 142–145, 178; "what is art," 143
Berg, Alban, 62
Berlioz, Hector, 62
Beuys, Joseph, 214–215
Bosch, Hieronymus, 151
Bourgeois culture, 94, 158
Braque, Georges, 140; *Man with Guitar*, 140
Breugel, Pieter, 151

Cage, John, 178
Calder, Alexander, 190
Carnap, Rudolph, 206
Censorship: in Plato, 53, 54; totalitarian, 163; recent governmental policies, 219–221, 238–239
Cezanne, Paul, 140; Bibemus Quarry, 140
Christian culture: in Hegel, 74–76, 79; in Schopenhauer, 114; in Tolstoy, 154–156; theology, 68
Classical culture, in Hegel, 74–76, 78, 140
Color, art of, 30
Connoisseur, 32, 94, 95, 100–102, 139
Constructivism, 159
Correggio, 126
Craft, 29
Creativity, 8; in Hegel, 84–86, 102; in Kant, 23, 25, 32–34, 37–39, 59, 60, 98–102, 112; in Schopenhauer, 56–60, 102, 104–106, 112–113
Criticism, 12, 13; "competent judges," 144–145; theme of, 157–163
Cubism, 141, 159, 234

Dada, 202, 203
Danto, Arthur, 202; Spoleto Festival U.S.A. review, 209–210
David, Jacques-Louis, 126
Delacroix, Eugene, 126
Depth psychology, 63
Descartes, Rene, 63
Dogma, 14; in Barthes, 164; nature of, 174–175; three dogmas of modernism, 171–188, 193; "expression" to "intention," 179–184; "progress" to "criticism," 184–187; "taste" to "form," 176–178
Duchamp, Marcel, 202, 203

Eastern culture, in Hegel, 74–77
Enlightenment, 48–50, 56, 59, 63, 68, 111, 117, 147, 226
Ernst, Max (*Immovable Father, Naturelle, St. Anthony*), 151–152
Expression, 10–13, 57, 60, 80, 89, 101–102, 109–115, 145–157; as modernist dogma, 179–184; expressionism, 141, 146, 149, 179–180, 204, 228, 235; abstract, 152–153; social uses of, 207–209. *See also* Schopenhauer, Arthur

Fauvism, 159
Feeling, 80, 82
Fiction, 120
Flemish art, 152
Form, 10, 12, 28, 31, 137–145, 152, 207; formalism, 138–142, 154, 160; as modernist dogma, 176–178; in postmodernism, 201–206; "significant form" (in Bell), 142–145, 178; simplicity, 202. *See also* Kant, Immanuel

Genius, 13; in Hegel, 84–86; in Kant, 23, 24, 28, 33, 41, 60, 98–103, 225–226; in modern-

ism, 181–184, 208; in Schopenhauer, 56–60, 114
Gilmour, John (*Fire on the Earth*), 214–215
God, 67, 68, 77, 79, 80, 82, 226, 228
Goethe, J. W. von, 82, 126
Goya, Francisco, 151

Hammoms, David (*House of the Future*), 209
Hegel, G. W. F., x, 1, 4, 31, 32, 38–40; *Aesthetics*, 70; art and nature, 70–71, 95; art and the ideal, 72–74; art and progress, 39, 84–86, 119, 123–125, 127–130, 158, 161–162, 177, 184–187, 212; artistic creativity, 84–86, 102; artistic truth, 118–120, 122–123, 232, 233; classification of arts, 74–82, 130; comparison with Kant, 63–71, 78, 81, 84, 89, 95–98, 102, 139; comparison with Schopenhauer, 44–46, 52, 59, 60, 63–71, 80, 81, 84–86, 102; dialectic, 69, 70, 128, 161, 232; evolution of spirit, 65–74, 102, 117, 229, 233; historicism, 59, 69, 82–86, 186; overview, 7–13; self-consciousness, 69, 71; social beliefs, 129; theoretical unity, 65, 122–123
Hesse, Eva (*Right After*), 217
Hesse, Hermann (*Magister Ludi*), 206
Holzer, Jenny (*Times Square Spectacolor Board, 1982*), 211
Horace, 81
Hume, David, 143, 145

Id, 148
Idealism, 3, 55, 66
Imagination, 28, 35, 82, 121
Impressionism, 126
Indian culture: in Hegel, 74–76; in Schopenhauer, 44, 51, 227
Ingres, J. A. D., 126
Intention, 11–13, 29, 145–157, 161; individual vs. group, 207–210

Jena, battle of, 125
Johns, Jasper, 190

Kandinsky, Wassily, 150
Kant, Immanuel, x, 1, 4; aesthetic system, 19–40, 121–122, 147, 180; "Analytic of the Beautiful," 92; categories, 21, 92, 143, 225; classification of arts, 27–31; comparison with Hegel, 63–71, 78, 81, 84–86, 95–98, 102; comparison with Schopenhauer, 41–51, 60, 63–71, 102, 104–106, 108; *Critique of Pure Reason*, 19, 20, 35; *Critique of Practical Reason*, 19, 20, 35; *Critique of Judgment*, 19, 21, 25, 105; good will, 34; moral freedom, 22; noumenal, 22, 41; overview, 7–13; taste, 89–106
Kiefer, Anselm, 214–215
Klopstock, Friedrich, 126

Landscape, 26, 27, 226; gardening, 29, 30; beauty of, 93, 94. *See also* Kant, Immanuel
Legacy: two notions of, ix, x; as thematic tracing, x, xi
Leonardo da Vinci, 80; (*Mona Lisa*), 203
Lippard, Lucy, 217
Literature, 29, 31, 61, 63, 64, 81, 82, 84, 107, 120; Greek drama, 126; Hebrew poetry, 78
Logic, 68
Louvre, 203

Madness, and creativity, 58
Mahler, Gustav, 62
Malevich, Kasimir, 162; (*White on White*), 158; (*Black Square*), 159, 202
Marxism, 68
Methodology, xii–xiii
Modernism, xi–xiii, 3–5, 14–16, 40, 57, 69, 76, 77, 84, 86, 89, 110, 113, 124–125, 127–131, 145, 149, 152–153, 157; comparisons with postmodernism, 191–192, 200, 210, 213–214; in Barthes, 165; radical sociology, 129, 157–158, 162–163; thematic analysis, 135–171; three dogmas of, 171–188
Mondrian, Piet, 141, 178, 202
Morality, aesthetic symbols in Kant, 38, 39, 97
Mozart, Wolfgang A., 81, 126
Museums of art, 94, 95
Music, 30, 61–64, 80–81, 107–108, 120, 126

Napoleon, 125
Nature: in Hegel, 70–71; in Kant, 26, 27, 63; in Schopenhauer, 45–47; and taste, 92–98
Neoclassicism, 36, 41
New Criticism, 164. *See also* Barthes, Roland
Nietzsche, Friedrich, 144, 148, 150; Zarathustra, 145, 215

Old Testament, in Hegel, 74–76

Painting, 29, 30, 31, 61, 79, 80, 120
Parmenides, 146
Picasso, Pablo (*Man with Guitar*), 140
Plato, 29, 38, 120, 122, 156; theory of forms, 52–56, 115, 150, 228; *Phaedrus*, 56, 115–117; *Republic*, 79
Pollock, Jackson, 180, 217
Pop art, 202
Postmodernism, xi–xiii, 14–16, 89, 131, 137; aesthetic themes, 201–218; criticism in, 212–218; form in, 201–206; intention in, 206–212; appreciation in, 211; history in, 214–215; legacy of, 189–221; memory in, 205–206; politics in, 197–200, 205, 216–217; popular art in, 213–214; programs of, 195–201; reaction to modernist dogma, 172–175, 187–188, 210–211; value judgments in, 196–199
Progress, 1, 10–13, 58, 64, 65, 68, 73, 84, 89, 97, 117, 119, 129, 157; as modernist dogma, 184–187, 193; in Kant, 96–98; in postmodernism, 206; in Schopenhauer, 228. *See also* Hegel, G. W. F.
Psychoanalysis, 116

Raphael, 80, 126
Rauschenberg, Robert, 202
Redon, Odilon (*Chariot of Apollo*), 150
Reinhardt, Ad, 202
Renaissance, 192
Rhetoric, 29
Rock music, 178
Roman culture, 79
Romanticism, 3, 41, 49–50, 56, 57, 111, 113, 117, 147, 179, 226, 228
Rossini, Gioacchino, 126
Rousseau, Jean-Jacques, 215

Schelling, Friedrich von, 110
Schiller, Friedrich, 110, 126

Schönberg, Arnold, 178
Schopenhauer, Arthur, x, 1, 4, 39; aesthetic system, 41–64, 122, 146–147; artistic creativity, 56–60, 104–106, 109–114, 149–150, 179; artistic value, 115–117; comparison with Hegel, 63, 64, 80, 81, 84–86, 102; comparison with Kant, 41–51, 60, 63, 64, 89, 102, 108; classification of arts, 60–63; overview, 7–13; Platonic idea, 52–56, 60; principle of sufficient reason, 44; will, 1, 8, 39, 41–45, 50, 106–108, 114; *World as Will and Representation*, 227
Science, 118
Sculpture, 29, 61, 78
Shakespeare, William, 81, 126
Skepticism: in Hume, 143; in Schopenhauer, 46
Sophists, 29
Soutine, Chaim, 150
Soviet Union, 159
Stalin, Josef, 160
Stein, Gertrude, 178
Stoicism: in Barthes, 166–167; in Schopenhauer, 46, 59, 229
Sublimity: and taste, 90; in Hegel, 77, 78; in Kant, 23, 25, 33–39, 77, 102, 147, 225–228; in Schopenhauer, 47–52
Suprematism, 158, 159
Surrealism, 150–152

Taste, 10–12, 23, 89–103, 138, 180, 225, 231. *See also* Kant, Immanuel
Teleology, 8, 40, 65, 82–84, 96–98; in modernism, 157–171; in postmodernism, 192, 199, 205, 221. *See also* Hegel, G. W. F.
Television, 206
Titian, 80
Tolstoy, Leo, 154–157
Tragedy, 61, 63
Trotsky, Leon, 160
Truth, 29, 42, 84, 118–120, 156, 232, 233

Van Gogh, Vincent, 150, 180

Wagner, Richard, 148
Warhol, Andy, 178; Brillo boxes, 203
World War I, 159; World War II, 164

Zeno, paradox, 194